NEW HOPE FOR BROKEN MARRIAGES

A BOOK OF ENCOURAGEMENT FROM PEOPLE WHO MADE IT!

Many Stories of Healed Marriages

"WONDERFUL"

"ANOINTED"

"INCREDIBLE"

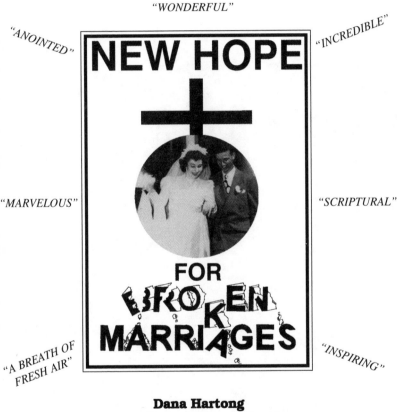

NEW HOPE

FOR BROKEN MARRIAGES

"MARVELOUS"

"SCRIPTURAL"

"A BREATH OF FRESH AIR"

"INSPIRING"

Dana Hartong
24652 Featherstone Road
Sturgis, Michigan 49091

269-651-2187

Second Printing $10.95

Drawings by Art Clifton

ISBN 0-9644136-0-4

Printed in the USA

Contents

Dedication

We would like to dedicate this book to the thousands of Christian men, women, and children who are adrift on the open sea, incredulous that they are the victims of divorce.

Acknowledgments

We would like to express our gratitude and thanks to all of those standers who gave permission to print their story in this book.

We would also like to thank Lynne Fisher for her excellent art work on the front cover. We would like to express our appreciation to Art Clifton for the fine art work on the back cover and for the drawings inside the book.

Foreword

*M*any of the marriage problems we are having in our society today can be traced to a movement whose goal is to reverse the male and female roles. We have forgotten that nature says, "The rooster has to crow." When you stifle the rooster from crowing, you will pay the consequences.

Men and women ARE basically different. Roosters and hens ARE basically different. Roosters crow...hens cluck. And when the hen demands the rooster cluck so she can crow, it spells disaster to our family units. There's an old saying, "When you hear a hen crow, there's going to be a death in the family." Today, hens are crowing and we are seeing the death of our families.

On the other hand, many times men have refused to take leadership in their home. They come home, sit in front of the TV and do not participate in conversation with their wife or their children. Sometimes it is nearly impossible to get Dad off "Dead Center." The husband is supposed to supply the needs of his wife and that includes talking to her.

Because the husband procrastinates constantly, the wife begins to assume some of her husband's responsibility in leadership. Soon, he abdicates the responsibility of the children, the finances, the home, the church, etc. to his wife.

The final result in that home is the rooster quits crowing and the hen quits clucking. Shipwreck of the marriage is the result.

There is HOPE, though. God gave it to us in His Word. The answer is in Ephesians 5:33, Living Bible. "Let the wife see that she respects AND reverences her husband — that she notices him, regards him, honors him, prefers him, venerates and esteems him and that she defers to him, praises him, and loves and admires him exceedingly."

Orders for the husband are even more demanding in Ephesians 5:25 and 33a, "Husbands, love your wives, AS CHRIST LOVED THE CHURCH AND GAVE HIM-SELF UP FOR HER. Let each man of you (without exception) love his wife as (being in a sense) his very own self."

When the husband and wife both obey God's rules in marriage, they get to reap the benefits and blessings, which are love, joy, peace, happiness and a one-flesh relationship that will never be touched by divorce.

Our goal in our ministry, New Hope for Broken Marriages, is to bring hope (desire, accompanied by expectation) to marriages that are considered terminal and to even resurrect some of them from the dead.

It is our prayer that when you read this book, it will bring New Hope to your Broken Marriage because:

BROKEN MARRIAGES DESTROY EVERYONE

Chapter 1

What Happened?

I want a divorce. I don't love you. I have never loved you. I didn't love you when I married you. I want out!

My pastor husband and I had been happily married for thirty years when he astonished me with this incredulous statement. I was in total shock and didn't have the vaguest idea what had happened to my marriage.

Many of you reading this book have heard these same words from your mate, and you too didn't have the vaguest idea what had happened to your marriage. That's what this book is all about.

What happened can be compared to having a physical stroke. One part of your body abruptly quits functioning normally. You signal your hand to pick up your spoon to eat, but instead of feeding you, your hand knocks your plate to the floor. You signal your leg to walk, and instead of walking, it kicks you. You tell your mate, "I love you" and in return you receive a look of hatred. You ask for a kiss, and they walk away. You are giving right signals, but receiving wrong responses.

Suddenly, there is NO communication with the person with whom you have shared your life for ten, twenty, thirty, forty, or even fifty years. You have lost your mate, the person with whom you could share your

1

dreams, your hopes, your needs, your thoughts. They UNDERSTOOD YOU. You feel like you are adrift on an open sea. You have lost not only your mate, but your best friend and confidant.

Before the stroke, your other half would take loving care of you. Now you are told, "Take care of yourself," with an added "You are not my responsibility." That is why it is so distressing and confusing. A person you could trust with your life suddenly becomes a person you can't trust with anything. That is why my daughter, Sue would say to me, "Mother, don't believe a word Daddy says". This was incomprehensible, because Dana had always been a person you could trust with your life, and his word had been his bond.

Now, he was not himself and you couldn't believe anything he said. I would look in his eyes and a total stranger would be staring back at me. I would cry out, "Where is my husband? I can't find him. I don't KNOW this person who is lying here beside me in bed." The trauma was indescribable. Our daughter Beth, summed it up in one sentence, "The person we are seeing is not our Dad."

Just as there is a cause for a physical stroke, usually the breakdown of an artery, so there is a cause for the one-flesh stroke. In Ephesians 4:27 the Bible says, "Neither give place to the devil." In the case of these one-flesh strokes, we have found that 9 out of 10 times pornography in one form or another, magazines, TV or movies, has opened the door for Satan to come in through dissatisfaction. When dissatisfaction enters in, the next step is deception, and then delusion. When you are in delusion the truth is a lie, and the lie is the truth. Adultery becomes an acceptable way of life.

Many Christians have become snared in Satan's trap by the acceptance of things they should abhor. There are many who thought they could dabble in porn, but they have come out the loser. When they dabbled in porn, they stepped on satan's trap. Amos 3:5 explains that "A trap doesn't snap shut unless it is stepped on." When a person is snared in this trap and it snaps shut, their mind goes "Tilt" and they are unable to tell a lie from the truth. In fact, deceived people BELIEVE a lie to be the truth.

Many times people who believe a lie enter into what is commonly called, "A Mid-life Crisis." I believe Dana's definition of a mid-life crisis describes it accurately. It is, "Rebellion against ANY restraint that keeps you from being what you think you ought to be and think you have a right to be, and rebellion against any responsibility that would interfere with that aim."

When a person's mind has gone "tilt," they are totally confused and completely unpredictable. One minute they will respond in a positive way, the next minute in a negative way to an identical situation. Dana told me one night during our valley experience, "Today, I love you, tomorrow I will probably hate you." He was right!!

When your marriage starts to disintegrate, you feel like you are walking on eggs with no solid ground beneath your feet. Your mind does the gamut of emotions; disbelief, fear, anger, pity, love, uncertainty, what's going to happen to me, not wanting to live, TOTAL frustration and trauma. You scream, "WHERE ARE YOU, GOD?" And then a beautiful thing happens. You finally realize that there is not ONE thing you can do to change your mate. You say to God, "Father, I give up. Do it your way. I take my hands off."

"Father, your Word says that you hate divorce, so I can pray according to I John 5:14,15 , 'This is the assurance we have in approaching God: that if we ask anything according to his will, he hears us. And if we know that he hears us — whatever we ask — we know that we have what we asked of him.'"

Since you know it is God's will to heal your marriage,

you begin to trust God's Word and hope slides into faith and faith slides into trust. Then, you know that you know that you know, I am going to be a whole body again. You are still one flesh with your mate, but one side is temporarily "Out of order." And, just because you have had a stroke on one side of your body, doesn't mean you cut off your arm, or your leg, or one side of your face.

You pray that prayer in Job 22:30 "Though he is not innocent, he'll be saved through the cleanness of your hands." Then pray Psalm 51:10 "Create in me a clean heart, Oh Lord, and renew a RIGHT spirit within me." Get your side of your body in order before the Lord, and then believe God's Word for the healing of the other side of your body. When you know that you know, that you know your marriage is healed then, "You do not fear bad news, nor live in dread of what may happen, for you have settled it in your mind that Jehovah will take care of you," Psalm 112:7. Psalm 118:7 tells us that "The Lord is on my side, He will help me."

Sometimes, God just goes ahead and performs a miracle as He did for Dana. God turned him around in the middle of the night while he was asleep. When I asked God, "What happened?", He answered me, "Look in Job 33:14." God can bring your mate home anyway He wants to do it. My one-flesh mate, who had the stroke, was well again. The only way God can control us is for us to get out of control. Sometimes desperate circumstances demand desperate prayers. Dana prayed a desperate prayer one Sunday morning when he cried out to the Lord, "Do whatever it takes, Lord, for my will to break."

I believe God's answer to Dana's prayer was, "Dana, I am going to take you at your word. I am going to allow you to go through a deep valley. That is the only way I can answer that prayer."

As we began the journey, I started to write answers

to my prayers in my Bibles, which were my constant companions. Several years ago I had a booklet printed called, "Through the Valley" which was a result of the notes written in the margins of my Bibles as we went through this valley experience.

So, we begin the journey through our valley:

December 10, 1978

"I want a divorce. I don't love you. I have never loved you. I didn't love you when I married you. I WANT OUT!!" My pastor husband and I had been happily married for 30 years when he astonished me with this incredulous statement.

January 1, 1979

God gave me Psalms 67:2, "I will send you and Dana around the world with the news of my saving power." This was fulfilled in September of 1985 when we received a letter from the Philippines. The people had seen our testimony on 700 Club and were praising the Lord for our SAVED marriage.

January 6, 1979

Exodus 14:14: "The Lord will fight for you, and you won't need to lift a finger."

Isaiah 43:2: "When you go through rivers of difficulty, you will not drown. When you walk through the fire of oppression, you will not be burned."

February 1979

Dana's anguished cry — "I couldn't survive without your love, Lord. Help me, I can't help myself. I am not myself." The Lord answered in Psalm 91:14, "Because he loves me, I will rescue him. I will make him great because he trusts in my name."

The Lord gave me Psalm 31:7, "I am radiant with joy because of your mercy, for you have listened to my troubles and have seen the crisis in my soul."

He said in Job 8:21, "I will yet fill your mouth with laughter and your lips with shouts of joy."

March 12, 1979

Psalm 94:17-18 says, "I would have died unless the Lord had helped me. I screamed,'I'm slipping, Lord' and He was kind and saved me." Dana had threatened suicide. He took his double barreled shotgun, started out the door, and shouted back at me, "I'm going to kill myself, and you try and stop me and I'll kill you." Since the Lord had told me, "Because he loves me, I will rescue him", I knew it couldn't happen so I just calmly replied, "If you have to, you have to." A supernatural peace flowed over me from God and Dana was back home in 15 minutes.

Psalm 90:15: "Give us gladness in proportion to our former misery. Replace the evil years with good." HE has and He did!!

Revelation 3:8: "I have opened a door to you that no man can shut." Psalm 71:3: "You have issued the order to save me."

April 12, 1979

Psalm 138:8: "The Lord will perfect that which concerneth me." Philippians 1:6: "He which hath begun a good work in you will perform it."

April 27, 1979

I told the Lord, "I need a miracle for Dana not to leave me." He answered me, "Write down what I am going to say. There are waves in the boat, but it will soon be calm. I have delivered thee. Dana will be baptized in the Spirit.

Pray that the eyes of his heart may be enlightened. I love you so much I died for you. I have a plan for your life which INCLUDES Dana. Keep the Sabbath day set apart. (This surprised me, it seemed out of context with the rest of what He said) He is still my man! I love him more than you love him."

Psalm 91:15: "I will answer him. I will be with him in trouble. I will deliver him and honor him."

May 5, 1979

Psalm 30:5: "Weeping may go on all night, but in the morning there is joy." Jeremiah 29:11: "For I know the plans I have for you says the Lord. They are plans for good and not for evil, to give you a future and a hope" (expected end).

May 11, 1979

II Chronicles 20:15, 17: "For the battle is not yours, but God's. Stand quietly and see the incredible rescue operation God will perform for you." I know, that I know, that I Know, my marriage is healed. Thank you Father, for my husband who loves me so much (I probably thanked Him 50 times a day).

June 12, 1979

Isaiah 43:19: "Behold, I am doing a brand new thing." Matthew 15:31: "The crowd was amazed when they saw the maimed, whole." Dana's right arm had been paralyzed since November 30, 1954 due to a corn-picker accident. This was 25 years later. When I saw this scripture, I exclaimed to Dana, "It says here, the maimed are going to be made whole. If you go to New Orleans, you are going to get a new arm." I knew, that I knew, that I knew he would. Three weeks later on July 4, 1979 God instantaneously and completely restored perfect feeling to Dana's arm. It was a miracle.

Isaiah 57:18: "I have seen what they do, but I will heal them anyway. I will lead them and comfort them, helping them to mourn and confess their sins."

July 4, 1979

July 4 At the International Full Gospel Business Men's Fellowship in New Orleans, Dana received the baptism of the Holy Spirit and the healing of his right arm-two miracles in one day. This did not solve our problems, but it was a means by which our problems could be solved.

Matthew 26:41: "Keep alert and pray." II Corinthians 4:18: "The troubles will soon be over, but the joys to come will last forever."

August

Dana asked me to please go and pick up the divorce papers, because he couldn't stand to see me hurt by having them served at the house. Isaiah 46:10,13: "All I say will come to pass, for I am offering you my deliverance, not in the distant future, but right now."

August 22, 1979

Prophecy by Harold Harding to Dana "The past is over and shall never be revealed. You shall be known as the man whom God touched."

August 30, 1979

Psalm 91:14: "Because he loves me, I will rescue him."

September 1979

Isaiah 61:1 (for Dana): "The Spirit of the Lord God is upon me because the Lord has anointed me to bring good news to the suffering and afflicted. He has sent me to comfort the broken-hearted, to announce liberty to captives, and to open the eyes of the blind."

September 8, 1979

"You are my beloved. Dana is my man. I'll never let him go. Just trust me. My ways are not your ways."

September 19, 1979

Dana saw an open Gideon Bible in a motel room. He planned to disappear somewhere in New England. The Lord had the Bible open to Malachi 2:14-16. This is what he read when he picked up the Bible, "The Lord hath been witness between thee and the wife of thy youth, against whom thou hast dealt treacherously, yet is she thy companion and the wife of thy covenant. For the Lord God says, I hate divorce." Dana was furious, and turned the pages where the same scripture leaped off the pages of the Bible. He flipped the pages again, and there was that same scripture. God had to rewrite the book that night, because that scripture only appears once in God's Word. After reading it three times, Dana jumped in bed and covered up his head and wished he was dead.

September 20, 1979

Dana came home completely turned around. I had my loving husband who loved me so much back home. I asked the Lord, "What happened?" He answered, "Look in Job 33:14." I answered "Why would I look in Job??" (Actually I was saying to God, You've got to be kidding.) God answered, "Because I told you to." To my amazement these are the words I read:

"For God speaks again and again in dreams, in visions of the night when deep sleep falls on men as they lie on their beds. He opens their ears in times like that and gives them wisdom and instruction, causing them to change their minds, and keeping them from pride and warning them of the penalties of sin, and keeping them from falling into some trap....yes, God often does these things for man...brings back his soul from the pit, so that he may live in the light of the living."

All during The Valley Experience, our children kept telling me over and over and over again, "Mother, some day you are going to praise the Lord that you have gone through this." It is now some day, and I do from the bottom of my heart, praise God that He did allow us to go through this.

Psalm 84:6 in the Living Bible says, "When you walk Through the Valley of Weeping, it will become a place of springs where pools of blessings and refreshment collect after rain."

I believe God allowed Dana and I to walk through this valley so that His plan for our lives could be fulfilled. Our testimony is a comfort to other people who are now walking through the same valley we walked through. Never in our wildest dreams could we have conceived of a ministry to help hurting people all across the nation.

We have printed thousands of our booklet, "Through the Valley". Every day we receive phone calls from people wanting "New Hope." As it has been said, "You can live without love, and you can live without faith, but you cannot live without hope." It is such a privilege to be able to give desperate people hope and to see their marriages healed. We are above all most privileged to be able to help in just a small measure those who are suffering from this plague of divorce that is upon our nation.

Chapter 2

My Part in This Mess

I'm leaving you, filing for divorce, and there is nothing you can do or say to stop me! Many of you who are reading this book have heard your spouse make this awesome declaration.

You ask yourself, "Where did I go wrong?" "What part did I have in this mess?" We pray this chapter will give you some answers to your questions.

It is incredible that in our nation 4,000 families a day go through the divorce courts. We live in a small mid-west town and just recently in our local paper the divorce decrees outnumbered the marriage licenses 66 to 47.

Our families are in a crisis. Divorce is an epidemic and it is urgent that we probe for an answer to this problem. Practically every person is affected in some way by divorce. We need to ask the question, "Why are so many marriages breaking-up?"

The obvious is not always the reason. There are always two sides to every marital problem. A lot of you have absolutely NO idea why your mate left. I had no idea why Dana had wanted to leave me, until one day we were talking to a stander and Dana asked her if she always had a better way of doing everything.

Suddenly, as if light bulbs exploded in my head, I saw myself as Dana saw me. I always had a better way of doing anything he suggested. And I was continually second-guessing him.

My comment was usually, "But wouldn't it be better if you did it this way?" Remember in the Foreword we said the rooster has to crow? By constantly having better ideas, I was usurping his authority and causing him to lose confidence in himself. He stopped crowing. I thought he had the problem. I found out part of this mess was my fault.

I talked to one lady who had no idea why her husband left her for another woman. One day when he was at our home, I got up my nerve and asked him, "Why did you divorce your wife?" His answer was short and to the point. "Because she didn't need me." He had gotten involved with a young girl who did need him.

A mature person is one who takes responsibility for their own actions and one who does WHAT needs to be done WHEN it needs to be done. But, by example we have been taught that if something bad happens to you, you find someone to blame and then you sue them. We have not been taught to say, "That was my fault", or "I can't blame anybody but myself." So, it is always YOUR fault, not MY fault. When you do this in a marriage you are programming divorce. We saw a poster on a school-room wall recently that said: "The only way you can fail is to refuse to take the blame." How true.

Have you ever given up your right to be right, or do you always have to have the last word in every conversation and every confrontation with your mate? This comes from our basic nature that cries out, "I can't be wrong. It's her (his) fault." We learn which buttons to push to infuriate our mate, and just sit there and push buttons. However, it is impossible for another person to make you bitter, or unforgiving. YOU are the only person who can make you bitter or unforgiving.

When a person refuses to take responsibility for their own actions, a powerful deception comes into their lives. It is always somebody else's fault when anything negative happens to them. Thus, every criminal in prison can say "It wasn't my fault. It was the way I was raised."

Their situation and your situation may not be your fault, but who you become in your situation is entirely up to you. When you face the fact you are who you are because of your reactions to what has happened to you, you have taken the first step to recovery. Learn to live by the Word, "In Everything Give Thanks: For This is the Will of God in Christ Jesus concerning you" I Thess. 5:18.

Sometimes you have to take a leap of faith in your marriage and trust God when you can't trust your mate. One lady, who had been married nearly 40 years, called me regularly after her husband moved in with another woman.

Her husband had lost his job and she was supporting him AND his girl friend. One day she called, really upset. He had asked her to withdraw their life-savings and give it to him. I was appalled and told her so.

But, "We'd better ask God what He says" I told her. As I was praying, I exclaimed "I can't be hearing from God right." God was telling me that this was a test. The test was, would she obey the Word that says to be submissive to your husband, or would she do what her flesh was telling her to do?. I sure didn't want to advise her to turn over their life-savings to her husband so I said, "I'm not going to tell you what to do, but this is what God said to me."

I never dreamed she would do what she did, but she took their life savings out of the bank and gave it to him.

Was it a test? Yes!!! She had always held the purse-strings and this was her husband's test to see if she had really changed. He left his girlfriend, moved back home and they have a wonderful marriage now. We get

Christmas cards messages saying they have never been happier in their entire life.

When your mate announces to you that he or she wants out, this is just the symptom of the problem. A virus is the cause of the problem. Just as a virus gets into a computer and wrecks havoc, so a virus gets into a marriage and wrecks havoc. When you have measles, the rash you see isn't the problem, it's just the indicator that there is a problem. The virus is the culprit. Just so in a marriage.

The problem in most marriages stems from the fact that most couples have the expectancy that when they marry, their mate will do for them what only Christ has the power to do. And that is the ability to satisfy and fulfill.

However, your satisfaction does not come from your mate, your satisfaction comes from Jesus. Your fulfillment does not come from your mate, it comes from Jesus. Your joy does not come from your mate, it comes from Jesus. Your hope does not come from your mate; it comes from Jesus.

When people begin to expect their mate to be God, this becomes idolatry. God says, this is sin. So, we have a virus in the marriage. Unless you abandon yourself to Christ and worship Him, instead of your mate, you will never be a complete Christian. This is not easy to do. It takes a mind change.

The same type of abandonment needs to be between the partners in a marriage, especially in the sexual relationship. Sex isn't the bricks of the marriage, but it is the mortar that holds the bricks together.

The problem is, there ARE problems in marriages and many times romance has gone out the window. When a man gets vibes or body language from his wife that says, "I'm only doing this to appease you. I really don't want to," he turns to imaginations. And pornography is nothing more than mental sex. IF a real partner doesn't fulfill all your needs, an imaginery partner will. The Bible calls this vain imaginations.

When a partner turns to vain imaginations, they begin to justify their thoughts (remember, it's never my fault) and they soon begin to live their imaginations. Vain imaginations always bring destruction. When this happens the man no longer tells his wife he loves her and can't live without her, and the woman no longer tells her husband he is the most wonderful guy in the world. (Ed Wheat's book, "Love Life" is excellent on the topic of sex in marriage.)

The relationship you have with your mate is a matter of attitude and body language. The vibes you send your mate supersede the words you say. If you never get around to going to bed at the same time he or she goes to bed, this is received as absolute rejection. When rejection comes, a lot of the time mental sex, or pornography replaces a loving relationship. Pornography is probably the most prevalent, addictive, destructive virus in marriages today.

When a man's ego is not energized naturally by word and deed and body language, the man turns to vain imaginations. And he has no problem finding vain imaginations. All he has to do is turn on the T.V. The truth of the matter is advertising works. So the Godly man has his eye drawn to women who are seducing men on some family sit-com and he is snared by the lust of his eye.

Because the man has not perceived himself (it doesn't matter whether it is true or not, that's how he sees it) as IMPORTANT to his wife, he allows himself to become important to somebody. Somebody has to want HIM, desire HIM, appreciate HIM. He is seeking the someone who will give him their undivided attention. That is why a man runs up thousand dollar phone bills to a 900 number. He wants someone who will listen to him and accept him just the way he is. He wants SOMEONE to tell him he is a desirable person.

Because this is all centered around the big "I", it is vanity. When you put together vanity and imaginations, you have vain imaginations. This is what the Bible says to cast down, not entertain. And entertain, they do. Mates who do not have five minutes to talk to their children, will set in front of the TV and watch porn movies until 4 or 5 in the morning. This generation that has grown up with porn as a regular diet, will reap the adage that says, "What you do in moderation, your children will do in excess." But, is it always the mate's fault when the partner turns to porn? NO! Porn is a spirit, and it transfers from one person to another, or from the TV, or from magazines to you. Sometimes it is there because of your upbringing. Our granddaughter babysat (once) for a 4 year old boy who got out his Dad's porn V.C.R's and tried to show them to her. This 4 year old is already hooked on porn. It is no surprise that his parents recently divorced.

The problem is, porn is the foot in the door for the destruction of the marriages. Porn, when it is entertained, takes over and controls you the same way alcohol, or drugs control you. It is addictive!

When people call us for the first time, we usually ask, "Was your husband or wife ever into porn?" We estimate that 95% of the time the answer is "Yes". Only the blood of Jesus can set them free from this virus. The Word says in Job 22:30 "Though he is not innocent, he'll be saved through the cleanness of your hands." You need to pray for yourself Psalm 51:10, "Create in me a clean heart, Oh Lord, and renew a right spirit within me."

Another virus is bitter-root judgment. This comes when you have judged someone for their behavior and said to yourself, "I will never be like that person." You have no forgiveness in your heart for them and you end up doing exactly what you judged them for doing. This happens with children of alcoholics. They become what they hated in their parents. They feel rejected and rejection brings low self-esteem.

A low self-image causes us to build a fortress in which we dwell, and NO one can get past our defenses, not even our mate. A low self-image exposes itself as cockiness, bravado, anger, defensiveness, sensitiveness, sarcasm, and sometimes withdrawal from friends and family. This virus of bitter-root judgment causes havoc. Only forgiveness of those you have judged erases it.

Sometimes the man has transferred his feelings of anger and frustration from his mother to his wife. His mother had corrected him, punished him, protected him, and had authority over him in his growing-up years. Now that he is married, he is supposed to be the head of the house. But he is married to a woman and how can he exchange places? The roles have been reversed.

Now, he transfers his feelings of unforgiveness towards his mother to his wife. The anger he felt toward his mom when he felt she was unfair, or partial to another sibling, or didn't understand his problem becomes enlarged. Maybe she never took time to listen to him or he felt he could never excel to her expectations. Now all this unforgiveness and rebellion towards his mother starts focusing on his wife. She can do nothing to please her husband.

I could do nothing to please Dana. During our valley experience one time he told me with a straight face, "If you're right you are wrong for being right."

A virus that is particularly destructive to a marriage is the Jezebel spirit. Since women are 80% more manipulative than men, it is something they have to fight all their lives.

The Anita Williams tape, the Jezebel Spirit, has been

a real help in understanding this spirit. Here are some of her teachings on this subject used by her permission.

"In Genesis 3:16 the Word says that the woman's desire should be to her husband and that he will rule over her. When the Jezebel spirit comes into a home, it reverses the order God intended for a marriage. It is in our nature to not want to submit to a man's authority. A woman who has a Jezebel spirit will be rebellious, controlling, manipulating, and dominating. The Word says rebellion is as the sin of witchcraft, and she will have a hard time receiving anything from a man."

"She may control with hostility, or she may control by emotional blackmail. She may blackmail by giving love or withdrawing love, by giving approval, or withdrawing approval, by putting guilt on her husband, or withdrawing the guilt. She has learned what buttons to push to get a reaction from those around her."

"God created man in his image, and since God inhabits the praises of his people, he created in man the need for praise. The way to a man's heart is not through his stomach, but through his wife's praise."

Ephesians 5:33 (amplified) says, "I will respect and reverence my husband. I will notice him, regard him, honor him, prefer him, venerate and esteem him, defer to him, praise him, and love and admire him exceedingly."

I remember one night I was lying in bed so angry I was just seething. I was so furious at Dana because I knew he was wrong about something and he wouldn't admit it. I told the Lord, "You know he is wrong and I know he is wrong, so why do I have to appear to be in the wrong?" I was so angry I got out of bed, went downstairs and opened my Bible. There staring up at me were these words, "Adapt yourself to your husband and do it willingly." I don't even know where that is in the Bible, but it is emblazed in my memory. I closed my Bible, went back upstairs, and said, "Thank you for my wonderful husband who loves me so much." Nothing changed but my attitude.

Anita continues, "Praise is what husbands thrive on, but be sure it is praise and not flattery. You can say, "Honey, you are so wise, you are such a wonderful husband, you are so strong, you are really a neat-looking guy, I'm so proud of you, I'm so glad I married you." Your praise makes him Your Prize."

"The Jezebel spirit in a woman causes a man to become spiritually impotent and sometimes physically impotent. When a man is emasculated, or impotent he avoids a confrontation at any cost. He becomes an Ahab. He says to himself, "If I confront her, I can't handle the situation, so I'll leave home. Or I'll escape my situation by sitting in front of the TV. Anita concludes by saying that the Ahab spirit brings destruction to the family unit."

A perfect example of the Ahab spirit is in I Kings 20:2,3,4. King Ben-Hadad of Syria sent this message to King Ahab of Israel, "Your silver and gold are mine, as are your prettiest wives and the best of your children!", King Ahab replied, "All right, my lord, all I have is yours!" or in our language, "Take what you want." Ahab had no spine.

The man is to provide spiritually and financially for his household. If he does not, the Word says he is worse than an infidel. What could be worse than an infidel? The only thing we believe it could be is that the Holy Spirit does not strive with them anymore. But the Word says in Job 22:30, "Though he is not innocent, he'll be saved through the cleanness of your hands." God's Word in Ephesians 5:25 says, "Husbands, love your wives, even as Christ also loved the church and gave himself for it." Husbands have a big order to love their wives as Christ loves the church. That means the husbands are to supply their wives every need, physically, spiritually and emotionally.

The Ahab spirit says, "I'm too tired, let her do it, or I want to do what I want to do, when I want to do it." Many times the husband has abdicated his position as head of the home. The "Silent Sam" man is as destructive to a marriage as a woman who never quits talking. A man does not supply his wife's needs when he will not enter into a conversation with her. Many times the wife needs to get interested in his interests. The Jezebel and the Ahab spirit are both rooted in selfishness.

Selfishness is the number 1 cause of divorce. It is also the number 2, 3, and 4 cause of divorce. When you prefer your mate, you are not going to do anything that brings them hurt. Wives, prefer your husbands! Husbands, prefer your wives! That will take care of the Jezebel and the Ahab spirit in your marriage.

Men and women call us all the time to complain, "But my mate is getting away with murder. (not really, just adultery) I'm the one who is hurting. He has everything going for him.

I hardly have enough money to put food on the table for the kids, and he takes trips to Europe, or Hawaii, etc. He seems to have friends, and his family is behind him 100%. He has respectability in the church. His girlfriend now has stolen affections from my friends, his friends, his family, the church family, and even friends where our kids go to school. 'She' even gets presents at Christmas from his family. Those should be MY presents. What used to be my circle of friends is now her circle of friends. I can't help being jealous and angry."

Dana always tells them, you only think they are getting by with sin. Just hold on. Obadiah 1:15 says in the Living, "Your acts will boomerang upon your heads" or as we would put it, What goes around comes around. God will take care of it. You have to forgive.

Unforgiveness is a destructive virus in a marriage. You say you can forgive, but not trust. Just remember forgiveness can come instantly, but trust takes time.

One lady told us that it took her 5 years before she knew with absolute certainty that her husband wasn't with his girlfriend if he happened to be a little late arriving home.

You can not afford the luxury of unforgiveness. So by an act of your will, will you make a quality decision and declare that you have forgiven? When you forgive, you never again bring the subject up, or by your body language demand a pound of flesh. If you do this, the pound of flesh will probably be your own. Remember, "Unforgiveness is like an acid. It hurts the container in which it is stored, more than the victim on which it is poured" (Unknown).

GOD ALWAYS SHAPES EVERY CIRCUMSTANCE FOR MY GOOD

Chapter 3

⌘

The Great Deception

A deception cannot be a deception unless it IS a deception. A counterfeit cannot be a counterfeit unless it IS a counterfeit. The Truth cannot be the Truth unless it IS the Truth. The definition of deception then is, "Deception is counterfeit truth which appears to be truth, but in reality is a lie."

So, how can so many Christian men and women hear a Word from God giving them permission to do things contrary to His Word? The answer is, when you are in deception, the truth becomes a lie and a lie becomes the truth. Truth is: The deceived are deceived.

Our prayer list includes many, many, pastors and their wives, elders and their wives, and church leaders of all kinds who are in sexual sin. If the leaders of the church can be deceived, it isn't long before the entire congregation is deceived.

One of the greatest deceptions we are being fed today is, "God's definition of marriage and the family has changed. It's not like it used to be." We have allowed our behavior to determine our definition and values instead of God's Word.

Andy Stanley, son of Charles Stanley, stated in his sermon on Family Values, (Tape MJ 182), "A family is a man and woman together for life, and if God so chooses children, biologically or legally by adoption. We can't change the definition of family simply because reality doesn't match up with God's ideal."

He goes on to say, "Single parents, don't allow our culture to parade you around as an exhibit as to why we need to change the definition of family. Why? Because God has already defined it. And what He has defined, we have no business redefining. God's definition of marriage is, 'One man for one woman for life. PERIOD!' " He adds, "If NO ONE in this country stays together, God's NOT changed His mind. and He's NOT changing His definition." (Used by permission.)

Yet, what is happening in our land today where over half of our marriages end in divorce? In fact, we had a seminar in one small town where the divorce rate was 83%. We were told of a factory there that had a reputation for destroying marriages. It seemed that nearly every person who went to that particular factory for employment ended up getting a divorce.

One of the employees, Jill, had just broken-up a home. A co-worker asked her, "Don't you care at all that he is a married man with children and grandchildren who are all being destroyed by this affair?" Jill flippantly answered back, "If I can get him, or any other man to LOOK, I just figure they are fair game and I pursue them until I catch them."

The enemy is seeking whom he may devour and he has covered our land with spirits of dissatisfaction, deception, delusion, adultery, enticement, bewitchment and prostitution. All of these are highly contagious.

Church leaders have lowered the standard, until divorces in the church are as great as, or greater than those in the world. As one person put it, "The wolves are in the sheepfold, and the way the shepherds are fondling them, you would think the wolves were the pet lambs."

We are sheep....We go astray....We follow the

leader....Out west the story is told of a whole flock of sheep who followed the head sheep over a cliff to their destruction. This is what is happening in America today. The sheep are following their shepherds over the cliffs. And...Broken Families Destroy Everybody!

God's definition of marriage is, "And the two shall become one flesh and never again be twain." Pastors say, "But God doesn't mean that....That is your interpretation of what God's Word means."

But, God does mean that, because He knows the consequences of what happens when you don't obey His Word.

Jesus says in Luke 16:18 (Anderson Bible), "Every man who divorces his wife and marries another woman is living with a woman who isn't his wife. And every man who marries a divorced woman is living with someone else's wife."

In Mark 10:11, 12 Jesus says: (Anderson Bible) "Anyone who divorces his wife and marries another woman is sinning against his first wife by living with a woman who isn't his wife. And if a woman divorces her husband and marries another man, she is living with a man who isn't her husband." I don't believe Jesus could get much plainer than that!

And, Paul couldn't get any plainer than in I Corinthians 7:39 where he says that a wife is bound to her husband as long as he lives. Only Death, not divorce can separate a husband and wife.

God's Word says in Romans 14:22, "Blessed is the man who does not condemn himself by what he approves for others." There are pastors who are not only condoning sin, they are indulging sin, and they are encouraging sin. Yet, in spite of what Jesus says in His Word, the clergy oftentimes make up the rules as they go.

According to information given to us by individuals with whom we have talked, you may divorce your mate and marry someone else for the following reasons...WITH the blessing of your pastor or your priest.

IF: You have changed any during the years you have been married. One man was asked this question by his priest, "Are you the same person you were when you married your wife?: Of course not! Then how can you be held responsible for what that man did. You are free of your wedding vows, divorce her and go find someone else." The priest went on to add, "Also, you have been defrauded because your wife is not the same person you married. In this case you have every right to divorce and find someone else." (Yes, this actually happened. We heard this same story from at least four different people.)

And he did

IF: You no longer love your mate. You are living in adultery if there is no love in your marriage. You need to find someone you are in love with, so that you can get right with God. One pastor suggested looking in the single's Want Ad's.

And he did

IF: After many years of marriage you become a Christian. Your husband still hasn't accepted the Lord after you have waited a whole year, then you have waited long enough. By all means go after that friends's Christian husband. After all, you did hear from God that you had a right to a Christian husband. So, go for it. Take him away from her. It's your RIGHT, because Jesus says you have a RIGHT to be happy. Her husband will make you happy, so do it and then ask Jesus for forgiveness.

And she did

IF: Your wife has become an independent person and really doesn't need you, or your income anymore, then find a woman who is very dependent upon you because a man needs to be needed.

And he did

IF: Your husband is not making enough money to satisfy the standard of living you would like, divorce him. After all, if he isn't supplying your needs, he is worse than an infidel. If he is worse than an infidel, it is your right to divorce him and find someone who is in a higher income bracket.

And she did

IF: Your wife is very ill and cannot go on medicaid because your income is too high, the only solution is divorce. Now that she is under medicaid, she doesn't need you anymore. This leaves you free to marry your secretary with whom you have been having an affair.

And he did

IF: You are a pastor and after many years of marriage you decide, "I should never have married this woman. My ministry has really outgrown my wife. I need to find a woman who will be a bigger asset in this position God has called me to shepherd. God has been telling me, that for the sake of my ministry, I have to divorce her and find a woman who is more on my spiritual level."

And he did

IF: You have been unable to have children. Discard
      your present wife and find a wife who can bear your
      children. You may have to find one who is divorced
      and already has children, just in case the infertility
      was your problem.

And he did

You are probably saying, "You had to make those
stories up. Those things just couldn't have happened."

But they did!!!

Part of the great deception is mentioned in Hosea
4:12 where the prophet says, "A spirit of prostitution
leads them astray." A description of what is happening
in our land today is found in Psalm 12:8: "The wicked
freely strut about when what is vile is honored among
men." Isaiah 3:9 says, "They parade their sin like
Sodom. They do not hide it. Woe to them. Jeremiah 5:31
tells us that, "The prophets prophecy lies, the priests
rule by their own authority, and my people love it this
way, but what will they do when the end comes?"

What is happening in our churches today? The same
thing that is happening in the world today. The only
difference is the location. Men and women are being
seduced in the bars, and men and women are being
seduced in the church pews. A friend of ours was sitting
with her husband in church one Sunday, when the Holy
Spirit revealed to her that the lady sitting next to her,
whom she had befriended, was seducing her husband.
And she did. Tragic!

The shocking thing is that it is happening to couples
who are 70 and even 80 years old. Couples are divorcing
after being married over 50 years. We know personally
a couple who divorced after their 50th Wedding Anniversary. This tragedy had a happy ending because they
were remarried on their 51st Anniversary.

In one church, there was a seventy-five year old man who was having an affair with a younger woman who had decided she was going to seduce him. When the gentleman's wife confronted his girlfriend and accused them of committing adultery, the girlfriend scoffed and said, "You are old-fashioned! There is no such thing as adultery anymore. That term doesn't exist." Jesus must be old-fashioned too, because He said adulterers will not have any part in His kingdom.

Church Leaders who are the best husbands and fathers in the world suddenly go "Tilt" and tell their wives they are in love with someone else. Because they love the Lord, they don't want to commit adultery while married, so they divorce their wives, so they can legally do what they want to do. They are so blinded by Satan that they don't even consider the fact they are breaking up two marriages with seven or eight children involved.

It has been common for husbands to come home and announce to their wives of many years, "I don't love you. I have never loved you. I have found someone else, and I am leaving you for Jane, Joan, Jill, or Joyce.

NOW, husbands are coming home and announcing, "I don't love you. I have never loved you. I have found someone else, and I am leaving you for Jake, Jim, John, or Jack. Sin is insane!!!

There are numerous men who were godly men who became friends with their secretary, OR a parishioner, OR a choir member, OR the choir director, OR the worship leader, only to become sexually involved. The end result is the shattering of home after home, and child after child. Many times these men feel more responsibility toward their illicit relationship partner, and often illegitimate child, than they do for their covenant wife and legitimate children.

The scenario goes something like this: "You have been a wonderful wife. You have been a wonderful mother. You have been a fine housekeeper and marvelous cook and I have had no complaints. But, I HAVE to leave. I know you are a strong person and you and the children will survive. I have a responsibility to take care of this other person. She is carrying my child...She needs me...." This scene has been played out to many fine Christian women across this land. Again, The Deceived are Deceived!

A born-again, spirit-filled believer, was seduced by his wife's sister. He ran away with his sister-in-law the day he was to bring his wife home from the hospital with their sixth child. He called her from a payphone to break the news to her.

A minister of music in a church had an affair, and broke up two marriages. He left his church because they were "mean" to him. His church wouldn't allow him and his live-in girlfriend to continue to minister in music. But, another church welcomed them with open arms, even giving him a title and position, knowing he was a married man who was living in adultery.

As one well-known singer put it, "It was like my brain was under anesthetic." A good example of a brain being under anesthetic was the couple we heard on a Christian talk show who said they were co-habiting without the benefit of marriage. Their solution was to pray out loud together and ask God to forgive them before having relations. They believed their prayers caused Jesus to sanction their sin.

Another church leader explained (with a straight face) his weekly adultery to his wife this way: "I ALWAYS ask God for forgiveness after I commit adultery. God has to forgive me because of His Grace. Things are just fine between God and me." This man is deceived, because it says in Jude 4b, "Grace is not a license to sin." Grace is a period of time when you have a chance to repent.

The road to this kind of twisted thinking we have been describing comes about very subtly and very gradually. When a Christian is first confronted with sin, he abhors it. Then, the next step is, he tolerates it. Soon he is entertaining it. The final step is, he embraces sin and calls sin good. When a Christian calls evil good he believes a lie and is in delusion. The only way out is through fasting and intercessory prayer on his behalf. The Word says in Job 22:30, "Though he is not innocent, he'll be saved through the cleanness of your hands."

We know even the very elect can be deceived and this happened to Kathryn Kuhlman, one of God's Greats. She believed counterfeit truth and was soon into deception. I am a great admirer of Kathryn, and of her ministry. But, as she said in her book, "No one will ever know the price I have paid to be in this ministry."

In his book, *Daughter of Destiny*, Jamie Buckingham tells the story of how Kathryn met this handsome, young, charismatic evangelist in Denver, Colorado. This was in the early days of her ministry and she and "Mister" as she called him, were holding meetings together. They soon became romantically involved even though "Mister" had a wife and children at home.

They were madly in love and made a striking couple. It wasn't long until he divorced his wife to marry Kathryn. All of her friends tried to talk her out of marrying him, but she felt life was passing her by at age 31, and besides she was in love with this handsome young man. She felt she could marry him and THEN she would ask God to forgive her.

Kathryn refused to listen to Godly counsel, and married "Mister" soon after his divorce was final. He justified his divorce by saying he had never been married in God's sight, (even though he had two children) and that made him free to marry Kathryn.

"In fact," he said, "Since he didn't love his wife, he was living in sin with her (his wife) and was just now repenting and getting his life straightened out by divorcing her and marrying Kathryn." Again, The Deceived are Deceived. James 1:14,15: "But, every man is tempted when he is drawn away of his own lust, and enticed. Then when lust hath conceived, it bringeth forth sin, and sin when it is finished, bringeth forth death."

When the couple told their congregation they were to be married, they pleaded with Kathryn, but she was a headstrong woman. In that moment they saw her stripped of God's anointing and she didn't even know it. She fainted halfway through the marriage ceremony, and "Mister" had to hold her up to say her vows.

Kathryn and "Mister" lived together for six years in deception and delusion. She thought it was better if people didn't know she had married a divorced man, so she tried to hide him, even denying she was married.

When she was exposed in Portland Oregon, the burden of guilt became unbearable. She got in the car and drove for six hours, weeping.

"I had to make a choice. Would I serve the man I loved, or the God I loved. I knew I could not serve God and live with "Mister". No one will ever know the pain of dying like I know it, for I loved him more than I loved life itself... I finally told him that I had to leave. The conviction of the Holy Spirit was almost unbearable. I was tired of trying to justify myself, tired...."

"One afternoon" she continues, the rims of her eyes brimming with tears as she talked, "I left the apartment and walked. At the end of the block I saw a street sign. It said simply DEAD END. That's when I died to self and surrendered to the Lord" She was confronted with Proverbs 28:13 every time she opened her Bible... "He that covereth his sins shall not prosper, but he who confesseth and FORSAKETH them shall have mercy."

She made her decision that day she walked down the tree shaded street and saw the sign, "Dead End." Three days later at the train station she and "Mister" said their last good-bye. They kissed and called caresses to each other as she climbed onto the train.

She never saw him again.

She went on to become one of the greatest hand maidens of God this world has ever known. Nobody but God knew what it cost her to be obedient to His Word.[1]

I have often asked the Lord, "How can people say they have heard from God and declare that He has told them to do something which is contrary to His Word?" One day as I was reading the Word, I found the answer in II Chronicles 18. When King Ahab asked King Jehoshaphat to join forces to fight an enemy, King Jehoshaphat replied, "Of course. However, let's check with God first." So, the king summoned 400 of his *heathen prophets.*They told the kings, "God will give you a great victory. Go for it."

But, Jehoshaphat wasn't satisfied. So he inquired if there wasn't another prophet of God around to get a second opinion. King Ahab angrily told him, "There is one, but I hate him. He always gives me bad news. But Jehoshaphat persuaded Ahab to go get Micaiah, the prophet of God. When brought before the Kings, Micaiah told them what they wanted to hear, "You will have a glorious victory." He knew they were deceived and wouldn't hear the truth, so he said it "Tongue in Cheek". But Jehoshaphat had discernment, and spoke sharply to the prophet Micaiah, "Just tell us what the Lord tells you to say." The answer was, "You will be defeated and King Ahab will be killed." That was not what the King wanted to hear, but he was seeking truth and his search was successful.

Many people who believe they have heard from God, have heard from their own lust and desires. They believe God has given them a Word to divorce their mates and marry someone else. Ezekiel 14:4 explains that God will answer according to the idols of your heart. Ezekiel 14:9 explains that God will even deceive a prophet to tell you what you want to hear.

How can YOU avoid deception? God's Word says in I Corinthians 6:18, "Flee from sex sin. No other sin affects the body as this one does. When you sin this sin, it is against your own body." James 4:7 says, "Resist the devil and he will flee from you." The problem is people don't flee from sin, they embrace sin. They don't resist Satan, they entertain him.

When people call us and say they are being attracted to someone other than their mate, we tell them one thing, "Put on your tennis shoes and run. When you get in a situation that could lead to compromising God's Word, RUN THE OTHER DIRECTION. And, USE COMMON SENSE."

If you are a single lady, don't invite a married (or unmarried) evangelist or singer to stay overnight in your home. You are inviting trouble. Never let yourself be alone with a married man. If you are a single man, never let yourself be alone with a married woman. God's Word says to abstain from all appearances of evil. You can save yourself a lot of grief by heeding this word from the Bible.

Ladies will call and tell us that it is the loneliness that they just can't handle. There's no one to ask, "How was your day?" There is no one to share your joy and sorrow with. No one to exclaim, "I was getting worried about you," if you are late arriving home. No shoulder to cry on when someone has hurt your feelings. There is no one to tell good-bye when you leave. You dread going home to an empty house where there is no one to greet you with, "Hi Honey, glad you're home." There's no one to share a meal, a hug, a story, no one to drop you off at the door when it is raining. And the list goes on and on.

When you consider the loneliness, it is very understandable that when someone at church, or at work, or wherever, starts noticing you, you become very vulnerable to deception. So, people call and tell us, "This man or that woman has been paying attention to me and it feels SO GOOD to have someone find me attractive and desirable."

When your mate has discarded you in the garbage can, and then someone comes along and treats you like an exotic dessert, *That is a heady thing — like high-octane gas.* YOU HAVE TO FLEE TEMPTATION.......
Maybe even quit your job, or change churches, or move. RUN, DON'T WALK TO THE NEAREST EXIT. YOUR SOUL MAY BE AT RISK.

1 Buckingham, Jamie. *Daughter of Destiny: Kathryn Kuhlman. Her Story.* South Plainfield, NJ: Bridge Publishing Inc. 1976. pp.

He's Mine! No. He's Mine!!

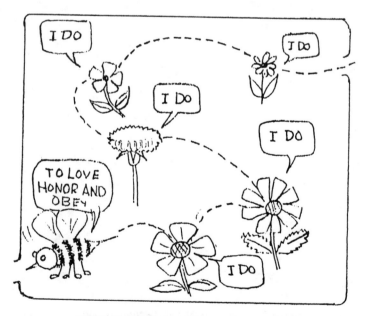

"Till Death Do Us Part . . . ?"

I'm Leaving You! I Have to Be Responsible. . . .

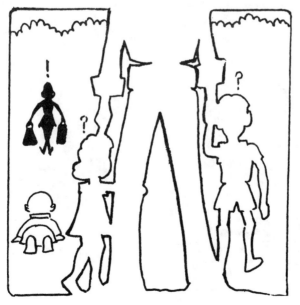

You Can Have the Kids. . . .

Chapter 4

Divorce — America's Only Legal Child Abuse

*W*hen children are neglected and left to fend for themselves, the world calls it child abuse. When children are subjected to pain far beyond their ability to handle, the world calls it child abuse. When children are emotionally crippled for life from parents who are alcoholics or on drugs, or who are sexually abusive, the world calls it child abuse.

But...when children experience these same emotions because of the divorce of their parents, the world does not call it child abuse. They call it "Getting on with your life." They rationalize, "The kids will adjust. Time will heal. They'll get over the hurt." But, will they?

Did you ever wonder why God says, "I hate divorce?" The answer is, He knows the consequences! God knows that each child is a product of both father and mother. When parents separate, their children are pulled in half. As one young man put it, "I feel like I'm the center knot in a tug of war. I feel compelled to be loyal to both of my parents, and feel like a traitor if I take sides."

The emotions the children of divorce feel are indescribable: anger, frustration, betrayal, hurt, rage, abandonment, neglect, dejection, desire to have things the way they were. They blame their parents and they blame themselves. One sweet little six-year old girl said to her Mommy, "If I kill myself, maybe Daddy will come home to you."

HOWEVER, CONFUSION IS THE MOST DIFFI-
CULT EMOTION A CHILD EVER EXPERIENCES.
When a family is going through divorce, the children
have no solid ground on which to stand. It's like an
inner-ear infection where you feel dizzy all the time and
everything just goes round and round. If you have ever
lost your equilibrium, you know exactly how a child
feels when he has been told his mother and daddy are
getting a divorce. They stagger around, unable to find
solid footing. Confusion in the spirit is like nausea in
the body. There are millions of children feeling sick at
their stomach, physically and emotionally. Their entire
balance system is off and the nausea just doesn't go
away.

The nausea hasn't gone away for a teen-age son who
reacted to his Mother receiving divorce papers by
yelling, "I'm going to find a gun someplace and go kill
Dad." She called us in a panic to pray someone could
find her son before he committed the act. The police did
find him and put him in a mental hospital. He didn't
need a mental hospital, he needed his Dad!

The nausea also hasn't gone away for a teen-age
daughter who had not seen her dad for months, and was
suddenly confronted in a Doctor's office by her dad and
his very pregnant teen-age girlfriend. She was inconsol-
able and threatened to do something violent. Children
just cannot handle the emotions that situations like
these trigger.

Millions of children in America will relate to this
poem that Billie Jo Atkinson, age 17, wrote about her
father out of her anguish and frustration. It is used by
her permission.

> There once was a house on a street,
> That slowly began falling to dust.
> If words are forever, and what you say is true,
> Then, how could you just leave us?
>
> Anger and hurt inside is only a little of what I feel.

It seems like you are playing with a deck of cards
That only you know how to deal.

Will the anger stay, or will it die?
How can I tell when all you do is lie.
It's like you are taking for granted the ones you once
*   loved,*
And throwing them all away like an old leather glove.

Not realizing their pain or hurt inside,
You are just hiding behind your own foolish pride.

Not only do the children of divorce have to suffer rejection, confusion, frustration, etc., they suffer humiliation. Most of the time they are left with the mother who suffers a severe drop in her income due to divorce. One lady called us sobbing. Her little boy was sitting at the dinner table when he looked up at his mother and asked, "Did daddy leave because he couldn't stand to see us starve to death"?

Now, children of "Christian families" are affected by divorce as much as children of non-Christian families. An example is a family in a western state. They had been a church-going family who did lots of things together. The father had been extremely involved in the children's athletic activities, and was a real family man.

His sister-in-law left her husband and asked his wife (her sister) if she could come stay with them for awhile. She was welcomed, but it wasn't long until she seduced her sister's husband.

Now they are living together in another city. There was no divorce and both mates are still married to their original spouses. Can you imagine the confusion in these children's minds? Their cousins are living with their father and their aunt. You just forget about having family birthdays and reunions.

The father is to get his own children every other week-end. But, he is so involved in his new life, he forgets to come get them. So, they sit on the curb with their suitcases packed, waiting on their Daddy to come.

But, Daddy doesn't come. Children forgive easily when Daddy says, "I forgot, I'll pick you up next week" but when it happens three week-ends in a row, this is cruelty and child abuse. The message they hear from their father is, "You are not important enough to me for me to make you a part of my new life." Is it any wonder the children are crying out for help by being disruptive at home and at school. They need their Dad!

Just the other day, I talked to a friend who teaches in a Christian school in Florida. She was relating to us how the children in her classes are hurt by divorce. She has two boys in her seventh grade class whose grades suddenly plummeted from A's to F's.

Knowing that the two families all went to the same church and were very active in ministry, she asked the pastor what happened to the boys.

The answer to that question was, the mother of the one boy got involved with the father of the other boy. Both sets of parents divorced, and now the boys are in total confusion. The couple who got involved are living together and the boys are torn with animosity towards their parents and towards each other. Their teacher confided to me, "I have never seen such pain, as I see in these boy's eyes."

The parents are scolding their sons, "Get your act together. Bring those grades up. This is your problem, not our problem. Such insensitivety from a parent is unbelievable, but it is played out in millions of homes across our nation every day.

Are they still all going to the same church?...Of course!

A friend of ours who idolized his father described his emotions this way, "The only way I could begin to describe my feelings when my dad walked out the door and left our family was it felt like I was following my dad through a mine field. He stepped on a mine, and was blown into a million pieces before my eyes. I stood there watching, helpless to do anything."

Our own son, Brad, couldn't bring himself to call his father, Dad while we were going through the valley. Brad would call on the phone and ask, "Is *he* there?" It took two years before Brad began to address Dana as Dad. But the day Dana threatened to kill himself, Brad was furious. He was here when his dad came back home. He grabbed the double-barrelled shotgun out of his father's hands, and snapped it in two over his knees.

Our youngest daughter, Jayne was teaching in a Christian school in Kentucky during the time we went through our valley. She called one day and asked, "How are things going, Mom?" It was not good timing because just minutes before Dana had asked me for a divorce. I answered, "Oh, just fine. Your father just asked me for a divorce." She slammed the phone down, jumped in her car and drove all the way to Texas before she stopped. She left her car at the airport, and boarded a plane to Washington state. We were frantic not knowing where she was. Eventually we found her, but it was trauma. She could not cope with her parents divorcing.

It is incredible how insensitive parents can be to their children. Several men and their live-in girlfriends moved into an apartment in the same neighborhood where their wives and children live. This is torture for the children who see their Dad with his girlfriend and her children all the time.

Contrary to what some of the experts said several years ago, a recent book, *Second Chances, Men, Women & Children a Decade After Divorce (1989)* by Judith Wallerstein and Sandra Blakeslee, has confirmed that the damage is permanent. The author says, "We were able to see clearly that we weren't dealing simply with young people going through the transition, but rather that, for most of them, divorce was the single most important cause of enduring pain in their lives." She asks, "Is it possible that the 'sleeper effect' a fear of romantic commitment, could plague them forever, or the lack of direction and 'sense of having little control over their lives' could permanently cripple them emotionally?"

The pain doesn't seem to mellow with age. We are acquainted with a man in his fifties who made the statement, "There isn't a day goes by that I don't think about my parent's divorce. I was about 10 years old when they divorced and they just split everything down the middle...including me."

We were talking to a lady in our church who is in her eighties. She exclaimed, "I still remember the pain when my parents divorced. I was 17 years old then and I still hurt."

Children's loyalties are like a teeter-totter between the parents. Parents are demanding that their children attend AND celebrate their wedding to a NEW mother or father. Sometimes they even demand that their child be in the wedding party. Many times if the child refuses, the parent will use bribery or blackmail. They are told "Either be in the wedding, or forget about your education, etc." Or, they are told, "You will never see me again if you don't come to my wedding." If this doesn't work they may use bribery. "Come to my wedding, and I'll buy you a car."

Children are a product of their one-flesh mother and father and they are ripped to pieces when they are forced to take sides, whether they are three or thirty years old.   It's like the children are the center knot in a tug-of-war between the parents. This tug-of-war can be for attention, custody, affection, loyalty, or as in most of the people we work with, morals and values. Children who are being raised with high morals by one parent are thrown into homes by visitation rights where sometimes there are bad morals or no morals.

One lady keeps calling and asking, "What can I do? What can I do?" Her husband takes their small children to bars on the weekends he has them. He also has remarried and has stepsons who are very mean and hateful to his own boys. Her boys are afraid of their stepbrothers, with reason. They have been physically harmed by them. Who does the father defend? Not his own sons. The boys are really hurting and are confused.

The article in the April 1993 Atlantic Monthly, "*Dan Quayle, You Were Right*" (Page 50) states, "Any event that permanently denies a child the presence and protection of a parent jeopardizes the life of the child. According to one survey, nearly half of all children in stepparent families will see their parents divorce again by the time they reach their late teens. Since 80% of divorced fathers remarry, things get even more complicated. Consequently, family disruption is best understood not as a single event, but as a string of disruptive events: separation, divorce, life in a single-parent home, life with a parent and live-in lover, the remarriage of one or both parents, life in one stepparent family combined with visits to another stepparent family; the breakup of one or both stepparent families. Given its dramatic impact on children's lives, one might reasonably expect that this level of family disruption would be viewed with alarm, even regarded as a national crisis."

When you realize that one million kids a year watch their parents split up, we ARE in the midst of a national crisis. The fall-out results from divorce are awesome. Pat Robertson made the statement on his May 12, 1993 "700 Club", that "Every act of violent aggression will spring somehow, from a broken home."

According to the National Survey of Children, in disrupted families only one child in six, saw his or her father as often as once a week in the past year. Close to half did not see their father at all in the past year. Ten years after a divorce, more than two thirds of children report not having seen their father for a year.

This survey doesn't take into account that not only do the children not see their fathers, many times they never see their extended family. Grandparents, aunts and uncles, cousins, friends, may all be lost in the divorce process. Children many times have to move to another city or state, and lose the home they have always lived in. When a child loses all their security, it is TRAUMA.

In the same article in the Atlantic Monthly, *Dan Quayle You Were Right,* (Page 71) Nicholas Zill states, "The evidence suggests that remarriage neither reproduces nor restores the intact family structure, even when it brings more income and a second adult into the household. Quite the contrary, step-families disrupt established loyalties, create new uncertainties, provoke deep anxieties, and sometimes threaten a child's physical safety as well as emotional security. One of the most severe risks associated with stepparent-child ties is the risk of sexual abuse. The threat of incest is 8 times greater from a step-father than from a biological father. It is chilling to know that 60% of American children will be a step-child by the year 2,000."

It has been stated that by the year 2,000 divorce will be the norm and staying together will be considered abnormal.

On a recent radio program, I heard this poignant story which illustrates exactly what is going on in the homes of America today. A 14 year old girl, Vicki Crosshire had written a little piece called, "That's the Way Life Goes, Sometimes." Listen to what she had to say.

"When I was 10, my parents got a divorce. Naturally my father told me about it, because he was my favorite."

"Honey, I know it's been kinda bad for you the last few days, and I don't want to make it worse, but there's something I have to tell you. Honey, your mother and I got a divorce."

"But, daddy!"

"Well, I know you don't want this, but it has to be done. Your mother and I just don't get along like we used to. I'm already packed and my plane is leaving in half an hour."

"But, daddy, why do you have to leave?"

"Well, honey, your mother and I can't live together anymore."

"I know that, but why do you have to leave town?"

"Oh,...well, I've got someone waiting for me in New Jersey."

"But, Daddy, will I ever see you again?"

"Oh, sure you will, honey. We'll work something out."

"But, what? I mean, you'll be living in New Jersey, and I'll be living clear out here in Washington."

"Well, maybe your mother will agree to you spending two weeks with me in the summer, and two weeks in the winter."

"Why not more often?"

"I don't think she'll even agree to that."

"Well, it can't hurt to try."

"I know, honey, but we'll have to work it out later. Now, my plane leaves in twenty minutes and I've got to get to the airport. I'm going to go get my luggage and I want you to go to your room so you don't have to watch me. No long goodbys either."

"Okay Daddy, good-bye. Don't forget to write me."

"I won't. Now good-bye. Go to your room."

"Okay, Daddy....Daddy, I don't want you to go."

"I know honey, but I have to."

"Why?"

"Well, you wouldn't understand."

"Yes, I would!"

"No, you wouldn't. Oh well, good-bye. Now go to your room and hurry up."

"Okay. Well, I guess that's the way life goes sometimes."

"Yes, honey. That's the way life goes sometimes."

Vicki ends her article about this experience by saying, "After my father walked out that door...I never heard from him again."[1]

When I heard this broadcast, I cried. I couldn't get the story out of my mind. Vicki's story was amazingly familiar to stories we hear every day from standers who call us.

A very dear friend of mine and her husband adopted a baby girl from Korea. The father absolutely adored his little daughter and the daughter was crazy about her father. They had a close, wonderful relationship.

When his daughter was about 16, everything abruptly changed. Suddenly he had a girlfriend, even though he was a born again, spirit filled believer. Satan deceived him and he chose the girlfriend over his wife and adopted daughter. His daughter told him, "PLEASE, PLEASE, come to my high school graduation, but if you have to bring 'Her', don't bother to come"...He didn't. The daughter has never forgiven her father and finds it hard to trust any man. Her own marriage will be affected by what her father did.

It is not just the fathers who are abandoning their children. There are many mothers who walk out of their children's lives to follow their own lusts. Four small children were standing with their father, sobbing as their mother packed her suitcase. She turned just as she was about to walk out the front door and said to her husband, as he was comforting their children, "I'm leaving you. I don't want the kids, you can have them."

More and more often we hear stories of women leaving their husbands and children. Their battle cry is, "I have to be me!"

I talked to a teacher from California, who told me that in one of her classrooms 98% of the children were from split families. The church is not far behind the world in divorces. For example, I was sharing this statistic with a friend in Kansas, and she said, "Well, where I go to church there are only about 10% of the children living with their original mother and father. Sometimes in churches the only couple not divorced may be the pastor and his wife. And.. there are many churches where the pastor, the elders, and the deacons have all been divorced. Many times the children don't have to worry about attending a different church on their Mom or Dad's visitation weekend. In these churches Mom and Dad have switched mates and everybody continues to attend the same church. Incredible!

One lady wrote me a letter asking for prayer and included a list of 30 couples who were either relatives or friends. They were all in the process of divorce, including the lady who wrote the letter. Can you imagine the confusion her children felt when almost every person who touched their lives was divorcing.

Several of us were eating at a restaurant after a seminar one afternoon. The waitress overheard our conversation and asked, "Would you pray for my kids? They are all having marriage problems." We told her we would be glad to pray for them and asked her to write their names on a piece of paper. She soon handed us a paper with the names of SEVEN sons, all who were in the midst of a divorce. The confusion of her grandchildren was indescribable!

We have heard many, many examples of mental child abuse from divorce. But we are living in a "Me first" society. Our nation is feeding on lust—lust for things and lust for sexual immorality. We have been tricked by Satan into a fast-food mentality that says: "I want it now. I can't wait. Nothing lasts, it's time for a change..." And we consider husbands, wives, children, and unborn babies all disposable. Now, even in the church you can get support when you say wrong is right, and right is wrong. But Romans 14: 22 declares, "Blessed is the man who does not condemn himself by what he approves for others."

One mother was asleep in bed and was awakened by the voice of her little seven-year old daughter. This child had gotten up at three a.m., gone into her Mother's bedroom and was using her phone. This is the anguished message she left on her father's answering machine in a city 100 miles away.

"It's the middle of the night and you are not home.

You never call me...You never write me...You didn't even send me a valentine...You never told me good-bye when you left..You NEVER keep your word."

"All my mother does is work, and it is all your fault. I WON'T accept a step-mother."

"I HATE YOU, AND I DON'T NEED A DAD!!!"

This impassioned plea received zero response from her Dad. How that little girl must hurt.

Jesus said in Mark 9:42 "But if someone causes one of these little ones who believe in me to lose faith—it would be better for that man (or woman) if a huge millstone were tied around his (her) neck and he (she) were thrown into the sea." We wonder if there are many fathers and mothers in America who have caused their children to lose faith by accepting divorce as the answer to their problems?

Could it be that many already have the millstone around their neck and don't even know it?

---

1. Used by permission
2. Taken from American Girl magazine copyright Girl Scouts of the United States of America. Reprinted by permission
3. Atlantic Monthly, April 12, 1993 *"Dan Quayle, You Were Right"* Barbara Dafoe Whitehead

Chapter 5

Every Circumstance Is Subject to Change

*H*ave you been waiting for your marriage to be healed and it seems like it is taking forever? Maybe you have been waiting six months, or a year, or even ten years. You agonize, "Will this nightmare never end?" You keep praying that all of this is just a bad dream, and you will wake up and everything will be back to normal. You can't believe that your marriage could ever be touched by divorce.

Take heart from God's Word that He shapes every circumstance for your good. God delights in doing the impossible. The Bible gives us many instances where things were changed instantly.

Remember the Disciples in Mark 4:35? One minute they cried out to Jesus "We are going to drown on this raging sea." Instantly, the sea was like glass. Jesus asked his disciples, "Where's your faith? Didn't I say we were going to the other side of the lake?" If Jesus directs your paths why do you doubt along the way?

You know you are going to get to the other side of the lake, because Jesus said so. You just don't know how!! When the waves get over your head at times, you begin to doubt that you can make it. But, in the first chapter of James, he tells us that a double minded man receives nothing from the Lord. So you can't afford the luxury of being double-minded. In present day language we would call it waffle-ing.

To make it to the other side, you REFUSE to look at the circumstances. You believe God's Word in I John 5:14,15. Those verses assure us that if we ask according to the will of God and He hears us and we KNOW He hears us, we have our petition. It IS God's will to heal marriages, because He says, "I Hate Divorce."

When you feel as if you are going to drown with every wave, just remember the words of Mrs. Booth of the Salvation Army. "The waters are rising, but I am not sinking."

Isaiah 43:2 tells us, "When thou walkest thru the waters I will be with thee, and thru the rivers, they shall not overflow thee."

Our problem many times is that we get impatient for God to work. We just don't know what mode of transportation God is going to give us for our journey. As one person put it, "When I started this journey I didn't know whether I was going to walk, ride a bicycle, take a bus, go on a train, or fly in an airplane."

"It has been eight years since I started this journey. My husband is back home now, and has accepted the Lord as his personal Saviour. He left the woman he had been living with and God is making him into the husband and father He planned for him to be when He made him."

This same lady told us about a dream she had when her husband was gone from the home. "I was walking down a hill and Jesus was walking beside me. I was enjoying His presence so much when He announced, 'I must set the captive free.' Jesus started walking ahead to what appeared to be a prison complex with barb wire and guards. The prisoners were pleading to be set free and their families were crying and pleading for them to come home."

But the prisoners were in chains and they COULD

NOT escape. Jesus walked toward them and then disappeared. As Jesus disappeared, her husband appeared. She then saw her beloved walking toward her. As she ran to embrace him, a knock on her bedroom door woke her. It was her husband. He had come home.

Remember Paul? In Acts 9, Paul was on his way to arrest every believer and have them killed, when Jesus stopped him in the middle of the road and turned him around 180 degrees. You may believe your mate is determined never to come home to you, and he or she may even have another person with whom they share their life, but then there is Jesus who changed Saul into Paul. God is in the people-changing business.

Dana was turned around 180 degrees in the middle of the night while he was asleep. He was planning on disappearing and never seeing his family again. He went to bed hating me, but according to Job 33:14, God caused him to change his mind in the middle of the night, keeping him from the pit. When he woke up the next morning, he was a different man and couldn't wait to get home to take me in his arms and tell me he loved me. Now, our marriage just gets better every year.

Remember the four men who carried their friend on a stretcher to see Jesus? They couldn't get close to Jesus because of the crowd, so they tore the roof off above His head and lowered the sick man on his stretcher right down in front of Jesus. And, because of THEIR faith (not the faith of the man who was healed) Jesus commanded the man, "Pick up your stretcher and go on home, for you are healed!"

Faith welled up in me one day as I was reading Matthew 17. It says something about the maimed getting new limbs. Dana had crushed his right arm in a corn-picker accident in 1954. His arm had been paralyzed with absolutely NO feeling for twenty-five years. I remember him asking me when we would wake up in the mornings, "Where is my arm?" He had no feeling of location.

When Matthew 17 became alive to me, I excitedly told Dana, "The Lord says you can have a new arm." I believed it without a single doubt. I pleaded with him to go to a meeting in New Orleans, where I knew the Lord would heal him.

Dana did consent to go to the meeting. Believers laid hands on Dana's arm which had been completely paralyzed for twenty-five years, and God instanteously and completely restored perfect sensation. One minute his arm was paralyzed, the next second he had complete feeling. Every Circumstance IS Subject to Change.

When we were in Florida several years ago, we talked to a lady whose husband had been gone 8 years. I told her, "Give me a call when he comes back home." She called me three years later and gleefully announced, "He's home!!!"

Ann's husband had been living with his girlfriend for 14 years. It seemed like there was no way this marriage was going to be healed, but then there is Jesus. Ann doesn't know what happened, or if anything happened, but one day he came home and he never left again. Sometimes we pray and pray, and pray, and then are in complete shock when God answers our prayer. Just don't quit. There is always hope.

Remember Jeremiah? Jeremiah was shut up in prison one day and set free the next. The captain of the Guard said to Jeremiah, "If you want to come with us to Babylon, fine, if you don't, fine. You're free to do as you wish." Jeremiah didn't even have to go before a parole board. He was set free.

A serviceman called his wife in the states and told her "I don't love you anymore, and I want you to get a divorce. I never want to see you again because I can't stand to be with you, so get the divorce and forget me."

He called her back the next day and told her, "I don't

know what happened to me during the night, but I went to bed hating your guts and I got up loving you. I can't wait to come home to you and the kids."

Again as in Dana's case, Job 33:14 was the answer to what happened to him. The last we heard their marriage was healed, they had a new baby, and they were serving the Lord together.

Jesus spoke to a husband who was on alcohol, drugs, and in adultery. God turned him around, saved his soul, and healed this marriage instantly.

One wife had not seen her husband for many years. He appeared one day out of nowhere with Christmas presents for the entire family. What did he bring them? BIBLES!! He had received Jesus as his Saviour and had returned home as the prodigal son. He and his wife were remarried on their twenty-fifth wedding anniversary.

Remember Lazarus? In John 11 it says that one minute Lazarus was DEAD,DEAD,DEAD, and the next minute when Jesus called "Come forth," he was ALIVE, ALIVE, ALIVE! You may think your marriage is dead, but at the voice of Jesus your marriage can be resurrected.

Mark 5 tells the story of Jarius' daughter. She was at the point of death and Jesus was on the way to heal her. He got waylaid on the way by the woman with an issue of blood and he took the time to heal her. I imagine Jarius was biting his nails about the delay, just as some of you are anxious and have been pleading with Jesus, "HURRY!"

Then the messengers came with the news, "It's too late. She's dead. Forget it. Go back home." But Jesus answered, "Don't be afraid. Just trust me."

"Just trust you!!!! Are you kidding? My mate is gone and my marriage is over. There's no way you can resurrect this one, Jesus. It's too late," we argue with God.

Jesus says, No, child. It isn't too late. It wasn't too

late for Jarius' daughter, and it isn't too late for you. The Bible says Jesus went into the room where Jarius' daughter lay, and said "Get up." She instantly rose from the dead. Jesus has the same power He had then, and He can raise your marriage from the dead.

One thing Jesus did do was to surround Himself with people of faith. He told everyone to leave except Peter, James, and John and the parents of the little girl. He told those who were wailing and crying to leave.

According to what we hear from our phone calls, many of you want sympathy for your situation, and you have surrounded yourself with mourners wailing over the death of your marriage. But, you have to avoid the voices of doom and gloom. If you want your marriage to be healed, you MUST surround yourself with people of faith who believe as you do. Don't ask anyone to pray for you who does not believe that your marriage will be healed.

Every circumstance is subject to change and Bob and Charlene Stinekamp's circumstances changed instantly. Bob was ready to marry someone else and God supernaturally healed their marriage. They now have a marriage healing ministry in Pompeno Beach, Florida called Rejoice Ministries. They are doing a marvelous work.

In California a husband who had been in a another marriage for 12 years came home. John Becker's other marriage didn't last that long, it lasted 16 months.

"Praise God, Donna waited on me" were the words John spoke to Dana and I, as he walked us to our car on his and Donna's wedding day, July 4, 1990. They had been through divorce and John married someone else. He testified that he knew the day after the wedding that he had made the biggest mistake of his life. He filed for divorce a few months later.

John just couldn't resist Donna's unconditional love. She sent him cards—so many cards that when they gave their testimony he had to bring them in garbage bags.

John couldn't bring himself to share Donna, his children, and his grandchildren with "Her." In his own words, "The entire relationship had been conceived in lies and deception, fed by lust, feelings of rejection, self-indulgence, a new life-style and new friends."

John and Donna were remarried exactly 35 years to the day they first met. John declares he wouldn't trade what he found for all the pigpens in the world. They now help other couples with marriage problems. Donna refused to give up on her marriage even though her husband divorced her and married someone else. John is so thankful and tells everyone "Thank God Donna waited on me and just wouldn't give up." What a privilege it was for Dana to help remarry them.

Just remember divorce is NEVER FINAL.

A lady called rejoicing that her husband was coming home after 25 years and two non-covenant marriages. She told me she always believed that her husband would come back home. She just never thought it would take this long.

Another lady also called to tell us that even though her husband had been gone from the home for 10 years, and had married and divorced two other women he had asked her to remarry him. God is faithful to answer prayers. Sometimes it is instant, sometimes it takes awhile.

Remember Jehoichin? In Jeremiah 52:31-34 Jehoichin went from prison to a throne above the throne of the kings in a day's time. What a transition! One minute eating food with prisoners, the next minute eating food with kings.

One lady hadn't seen her husband for months. He showed up one holiday, rode in a float in a parade with her that day, and has been home ever since. She told me some of her friends were standing along the sidewalk watching the parade go by. When they saw her husband on the float with her, they just stood there with their mouth open. They had been believing with her for the healing of her marriage. But when they saw it, they couldn't believe it. God delights in surprising people.

Remember the story of the mad man of the Gadarenes? This man lived among the gravestones and had such strength that whenever he was chained, he snapped the chains and walked away. All day and all night he would wander among the tombs screaming and yelling and cutting himself with sharp stones.

Then he saw JESUS! He fell down before Him and worshipped Him. One minute he was insane, the next minute he was in his right mind. This man left Jesus and went all over the countryside proclaiming the wonderful thing Jesus had done for him and all men did marvel.

If this had happened today, all of his wife's friends would have been advising her, "Divorce him and go find someone else. You have a RIGHT to happiness. He's insane and his condition is never going to change. Your marriage is hopeless." They don't consider the power of Jesus to change men.

You say, "That sounds like my husband or wife. They really are not in their right mind." The answer is, "That's right. They are not in their right mind because...Sin is Insane. They are acting perfectly normal for someone controlled by Satan."

Pastors, elders and other leaders who were appalled by sin are now openly flaunting sin. The reason...sin IS insane. They are not in their right mind. They have been deceived and deluded. And....Satan has set a trap and snared them.

One lady had a vision of Dana while we were going through the valley. She saw him completely encased with a fish net made of inch-thick rope. But there was an angel of the Lord standing over him with a sword getting ready to cut him out and set him free. That is exactly what happened. He was instantly set free that September night. God can set your mate free from the snare of Satan.

Sherri and her husband were youth leaders in a large church. Sherri had always loved the Lord and the desire of her heart was to serve Him. But, she got into deception by listening only to counselors who would tell her what she wanted to hear. She divorced her husband, and married someone else.

We had been standing with her husband for the healing of this marriage. One day I prayed, "Lord just tear the veil from her eyes!" She was sitting at her desk at work when her husband walked in to talk to her about their children. She looked up at him and exclaimed, "I'm living in adultery." She called to tell me that it felt like a veil had been torn from her eyes. She immediately filed for divorce and reconciled with the husband of her youth.

Remember Mordecai? What goes around comes around. Haman had a plot to destroy Mordecai and all the Jews. He built a gallows to hang Mordecai on. But Esther fasted and prayed and intervened with the King. Instead of Mordecai being the one to hang on the gallows, Haman was hung on the gallows.

One minute Haman was second in command in the land, the next minute he was dead. The plot that Mordecai believed would kill him, turned around and blessed him. One minute he faced the hangman's gallows, the next minute he became a leader in his land. God shapes every circumstance for our good, even the bad circumstance.

This was going to be the wedding of her dreams. Ruth was almost 40 years old. She had waited a long time for Mister Right to come along. Finally, she was convinced, God had answered her prayers. There was a little problem though. Her fiance had been married before.

But after asking several pastors and counselors, she was certain she had God's blessing to go ahead with wedding plans. So the date was set and all the wedding arrangements were made. The entire congregation entered into making this wedding day a day to remember.

But, Ruth had a friend who believed marriage was for life. This friend was waiting for her own husband to return home. She explained to Ruth that she loved her, but she could not put her stamp of approval on this marriage by attending. She explained to her that it would be adultery because he has a living wife.

Ruth was very upset, but she really loved the Lord so she told her friend, "I won't cancel the wedding. I can't back out now, but if you are right and it isn't God's Will for me to marry this man, He will have to cancel it."

The wedding WAS canceled a week before it was to take place. I'm sure the man's wife, who had been waiting for her husband to come home, considered this a miracle.

While you are waiting for the healing of your marriage, you have to remember, EVERY CIRCUMSTANCE IS SUBJECT TO CHANGE. Sometimes it is gradual, sometimes it happens in an instant. Just remember, God hasn't forgotten you, and as HE says, "I Will Watch Over My Word to Perform It" Jeremiah 1:12.

I asked for permission from Tina and Terry to include their story in our book. It is one of the best examples I have ever heard that explains how, "Every Circumstance is subject to change." God does change people's will. They asked that I use their real names.

Tina tells the story: "After six and a half years of marriage, I WANTED OUT! I felt like Terry was so busy doing things with other people, that he had no time for me. I believed my husband was my enemy. We had absolutely no communication and I felt nothing but rejection from him. At the same time he was feeling nothing but rejection from me."

"I finally had all I could take and on February 2, 1988 I made Terry leave our home. I prayed and I honestly felt 'divorce' was what God wanted. After talking to a pastor, I was sure this was what God wanted. I sought God daily, and would read scriptures and use my own interpretation to do what I wanted to do."

"During the summer of 1988, I started dating. I was convicted of what I was doing and where I was going. But, I saw other Christians doing the same thing, and I thought if they could do it and still be a Christian, why couldn't I? This was the excuse I used, even though I knew what I was doing was wrong."

"Terry constantly reminded me I was his wife and he wouldn't agree to a divorce. After stalling as long as he could, the divorce finally went through and I received custody of our two girls."

"I was lonely and miserable, but I told everybody I was happy the way things were going, and there was no way I would ever go back to Terry, I never loved him. Terry wanted to give up on our marriage, but our two small daughters, Tasha and Tristan, just kept repeating,'We have to be a 'FLAMILY' again!'"

"Everytime Terry would pick up the girls for visitation, we would argue. He would leave hurt, angry and lonely. The littlest things would make me mad when he would come, whether it was the way he dressed, the way he combed his hair, his walk, or just anything. We went to court a second time because Terry believed God had told him to go to court to get custody of the girls. To my shock, he did receive custody. I thought I would literally die without my children."

"I was supposed to be married in a few weeks, but if somebody or anybody would have told me, `You shouldn't marry this man, I wouldn't have.' He was supposed to be a Christian, but he was a very abusive person."

"After two weeks of marriage, I told him to leave and I filed for divorce. In the meantime, I found out I was pregnant by this man."

"My mother's advice for the whole situation was, 'Pray for a love for Terry.' At first, I thought she was crazy, but I decided to try it. What did I have to lose? I had to literally make myself pray this way and really mean what I was praying. I had NO desire to do this, and prayed only for just enough love to tolerate Terry, since we had to communicate regarding the girls."

"On June 30th, I started looking at some old family pictures. Terry was in several of them and I started missing him. I couldn't believe it. That night I woke up twice crying out to God telling Him I didn't want my marriage back together, and how could that be His perfect will?".

"The next day I called Terry and when he answered the phone I burst into tears. Through sobs I asked him if God had been dealing with him over the weekend. 'NO', he vehemently answered, 'He's been dealing with me the WHOLE TIME we were apart, to stand for my marriage'. I told him I had prayed to have a love for him, but God was giving me so much love for him, that I missed him terribly and I had to see him right away. As I heard these words tumble out of my mouth, I couldn't believe it was me saying them."

"Even though I was pregnant with another man's child, Terry couldn't wait to remarry me. The children couldn't wait to be a 'Flamily' again. The divorce finally became final on December the sixth, and on December the seventh 1989 at one minute after midnight Terry and I were remarried. The baby was born the same day at 9:24 a.m. So, in twenty-four hours I was divorced, remarried and gave birth to a baby boy."

"Terry wanted to name the baby Terynce Jr. after him, and we did. We also prayed that Terry, Jr. would have no features of his birth father and he doesn't. He looks more like Terry than our other children. What a miracle!"

"I thank God that Terry stood for our marriage. I praise God our two precious little girls stood for our marriage even when I told them to forget it. I can't praise and thank God enough that we truly are a 'Flamily' again."

"Not only has God restored our marriage, he has given us the privilege of working with other couples in the restoration of their marriage. We praise God for the opportunity of helping others through our testimony."

Just remember, divorce is NEVER final because EVERY Circumstance is Subject to Change.

Chapter 6

Unconditional Love

*I*f you love someone unconditionally, you want to say and do things that will please them, make them happy, comfortable, secure, content, joyful, thankful.

If you don't love someone unconditionally, you're happy when they hurt, glad when bad things happen to them, and gleeful when troubles come and they get what you think they deserve.

But, we are to love unconditionally the way Jesus loves us. When we do that, our love is not dependent upon anything our mate says, or doesn't say, and it is not dependent upon anything our mate does, or doesn't do.

Your spouse has to KNOW, that they KNOW, that they KNOW, "Hey, I'm on YOUR Side". It is not me against you, it's us against the enemy. I can't tell you how to accomplish this. It is something that comes across in tone of voice, inflection of words, your reactions to situations, and what is inside of you exposing your true feelings and thoughts. In other words, it's your body-language.

Many couples never have the confidence of knowing and understanding that oneness which comes from a one-flesh relationship that says, "We're in this thing together." Instead, when natural disasters come or oftentimes the death of a child, parents divorce. The enemy uses such things as Hurricane Andrew, the Mississippi flood of 1993, and the earthquake in California to drive a wedge between couples. The reason for the rash of divorces after these disasters is the mates are not convinced that they are on each other sides.

The very things which should cause us to lean toward each other and unify our strength to overcome adversity, defeat us. The answer is, we do not have the sense of one-flesh and common purpose.

In unconditional love, you give up the right to be right. Dana once told me, when we were going through the valley, that if I was right, I was wrong for being right. He wasn't joking, either. He meant it!

If you are right, sooner or later you are going to be proven right. If you are wrong, be glad you didn't insist that you were right.

I don't know who penned these words, but everyone of our children can quote them. We admonished them over and over and over again, "He who defends his honor, soon has no honor to defend." The Lord is your defense and if you insist on interrupting and defending yourself, God will tell you that if you would rather do it yourself, you don't need His help. But, if you will give it to Him, and leave it with Him, HE will shape every circumstance for your good, because He does all things well.

You can not have a good marriage without being vulnerable to each other. Being vulnerable means you hand over a weapon to your mate with which they could, if they desired, destroy you. You have to trust each other with your lives. You also have to take risks in a marriage. You take the risk of being misunderstood or used.

A lot of people call us and bemoan, "But, we're SICK of being used." I was talking to Jesus one morning and complaining, "I am SICK of being used". He answered me back instantly, "Are you any better than I am?" I was so shocked at His answer, I never again repeated that phrase. "No, Lord I surely am not better than you. I will rejoice when I am used from now on. I have prayed to be more like you and the only way I can be more like you is to be USED with unconditional love. So...Use Me."

A lady whom I admire very much, called to update us last week. Her husband has been gone four years and is living with another woman. She loves him with no conditions. He had been a fine Christian man, but had gotten caught in the lust trap. He loves his wife and comes to visit every few weeks and sometimes they have relations. He has never filed for divorce. My friend's family and friends are outraged. They tell her, "You are nothing but a doormat for that man." She has the best rebuttal for that I have ever heard. "Yes, I am! And my doormat has always said, WELCOME!!!!" She KNOWS her unconditional love will triumph.

Unconditional love is simply love with no conditions. It doesn't matter what you do, or what you say, I am going to love you. This is not an easy thing to do. It takes prayer and sometimes even fasting.

You have to surrender yourself and your mate to God. You can even rejoice when fiery trials come, like His Word says to do. It can not be done in the flesh, because our flesh screams, "I can't take this. I want out of this pain and distress." But Paul says, I can do ALL things through Christ who strengthens me. And, YOU CAN TOO. You just determine you have NO Other Option, but to stand for your marriage.

The first truth you have to accept when you begin your stand for your marriage, is that YOU cannot change your husband or wife. The ONLY person you can change is yourself. So, begin praying, "Lord, change me. Make me into the wife or husband you planned for me to be when you made me. Show me what you want to change in my life and please do it. I give you permission to change my attitudes, my desires, my thoughts, my body language, my reactions, my commitment. Line me up with YOUR WORD. I WILL give thanks in everything, for this is the will of God in Christ Jesus concerning me.

I thank you that you are making my mate into the person you planned them to be when you made them. I praise you that you are changing them into the person I have prayed for them to be. I know that only 10% of what has happened to me has made me into the person I am today. How I reacted to my circumstances is 90% of what has made me who I am today.

I know it has to be the sails that set my course, NOT the gales. So...I surrender to You, Father. I surrender my mate to you, Father. I surrender my marriage to you and I promise not to interfere while you heal us and make our family into the family you planned it to be."

A proven truth is that carnal weapons absolutely will not work. I am sure you have found that threats, manipulations, accusations, tongue-lashings. imposing guilt, withdrawing your spirit, withdrawing your body, seeking revenge has not worked. Neither does issuing ultimatums such as, "You walk out that door and I file for divorce." When you try and do what you think God isn't getting done, all you get is bruises.

What does work is the Word of God. Jesus says we have to use spiritual weapons to fight spiritual battles. For the weapons of our warfare are not carnal, they are mighty to the pulling down of strongholds. Some of our weapons are: standing on the Word of God with absolute confidence God will do what He says He will do, prayer and fasting, faith, truth, trust, pleading the blood of Jesus over our mates, anointing our homes with oil, changing our vision of reality from what we see to what God says, forgiveness and unconditional love.

For example, when Dana would say, "I don't love you anymore", I would tell God, "Thank you for my husband who loves me so much." When he told me he had filed for divorce, I said to God, "Thank you Father, that my marriage is healed" I believed what God said, not what Dana said.

Here are some stories of unconditional love and how it worked in the lives of these standers. Their marriages were healed and yours can be too, with Jesus' love. I have changed their names and a few details.

Ellen had been believing God for her marriage for four years. She would call us nearly every week just to be encouraged. We call ourselves cheerleaders for marriages and we try and hold up the arms that hang down from discouragement. We would have liked to have told her at times "Leave him, he's not worth it." But we never want to counsel contrary to God's Word, so we would always say,"Hang in there, you are going to make it". And she did. But not without much pain and tears.

She REFUSED to look at the circumstances. She stood on the scripture in I John 5:14, 15 that says in the Amplified Version of the Bible, "And this is the confidence, the assurance, the (privilege of) boldness which we have in Him: (we are sure) that if we ask anything (make any request) according to His will (in agreement with His own plan) He listens to and hears us. And if (since) we (positively) know that He listens to us in whatever we ask, we also know (with settled and absolute knowledge) that we have (granted us as our present possession) the requests made of Him." Since God says He hates divorce, she had no problem believing that God had heard her prayer and that her marriage was healed.

Ellen shared her husband with his girlfriend for three of those four years. Lester would spend 4 nights a week with his friend and three nights a week with his wife. Ellen never accused him, she just loved him. She was devastated by his actions, but she believed God's Word, not what she saw. She would write him love notes and put them in his lunch sack. She would leave love notes under his pillow. She would buy cards and put them in his vehicle.

One evening around five o'clock he called and said he would be right home. They were going to have their Thanksgiving meal. She waited and waited, trying to keep the food hot. Finally, around 11 o'clock he showed up.

She asked, "Would you like something to eat, I've been saving it for you." (In a later conversation with Ellen, she admitted that she really wanted to *throw* the turkey at him instead of serving it to him. But she had called us several times that day and Dana always told her, "Hold Steady."

They sat down and ate a holiday meal. And as they were eating, Lester tearfully asked. "Why do you love me, when you know what I'm doing?" She replied, because you are a good man. You are a kind man. You are a good provider. You are a good father. You are a good husband. And she went on to list other wonderful attributes of her husband.

The next morning, she said to herself, I bet he would like to have that in writing. So, she wrote him a note and told him she was writing it all down for him, so he could have it to read. She put it in an envelope and placed it in his truck. She really loved that man with an unconditional love, expecting nothing in return.

If Ellen would have looked at Lester with her carnal eyes, she would have seen a man who was betraying his wife, children, grandchildren and Jesus. But, she saw him with her spiritual eyes. She saw him as a wonderful husband, father, grandfather and man of God. He became what she saw.

When Lester found the love note in his truck, that was the turning point. He began to come home the nights he usually spent with his girlfriend. Soon he was home to stay. Ellen called one day to tell us that she had never known such happiness. She laughed and said, "My kids tell us we embarrass them because we act like we're on a perpetual honeymoon."

After he had been home about a year, Lester whispered as he held Ellen in his arms, "Thank God, you waited on me." She tearfully answered him with a smile, "I would have waited forever."

When I called to ask permission to put their story in this book, I asked Ellen, "Now that you have been back together for several years, how are things?" Her voice had a lilt as she answered me, "Things just COULDN'T be any better. The praise goes to God."

In a few weeks, we received a note thanking us for including their story in our book. She said, "I remember the night I made that turkey dinner and waited and waited and waited for Lester to come home. You are right, that was the turning point. As I said before, I have to tell you the temptation was great that night to throw the turkey at him, instead of feeding it to him. But, I remembered Dana's counsel to just love him and since that night, we couldn't be any happier."

I can hear you say as you are reading this story, "That woman was crazy. I could never do that." No, YOU couldn't do that. But, Jesus living in you could do that because that is the way Jesus loves us now, with an unconditional love.

Helen had a really rough time in her marriage. Her husband was on dope, drinking alcohol and living with another woman with whom he had had 2 children. The only time he would come home would be when Helen was at work. He would take the TV or anything that he could sell to get money. He even took the food out of the refrigerator. He left her with house payments, car payments, furniture payments, and no money to pay bills.

He would bring his illegitimate children over and taunt Helen because she was unable to have children.

She always answered back with unconditional love and would take his children to church with her.

We told her once on the phone, "If we would tell you what we would like to tell you, we would tell you to get rid of him, he is no good." We were especially angry at him the day she called crying. She had a package of lunchmeat in the refrigerator which was all she had to eat for the next week. He came to the house while she was at work and took it.

That was the day Dana advised her, "I'd change the locks on the house." He called her back the next day and told her, "I was getting too sympathetic. Forget what I told you yesterday." She laughed and said, "I knew you didn't mean it. You just felt sorry for me. I didn't change them."

Helen refused to look at her circumstances. She would declare to us, "I know there is a good man in there someplace. When God gets hold of him, he is going to be something else."

God did get hold of him and Helen's husband was transformed into the husband of her dreams. Not only that, but God performed another miracle. The Doctors had declared there was no way Helen could ever get pregnant. But, then there is God. After 13 years of marriage, a beautiful baby was born to this couple. We were privileged to meet Helen's transformed husband and new little baby girl. Now, Helen and her husband take their baby and his children by his girlfriend to church every Sunday. This is truly unconditional love.

And then there was John, whose wife had left him. She had been living with another man for 6 years. He would call and say, "She won't have anything to do with me, she won't even let me touch her hand. You can't believe how easy it would be for me to find a woman to move in with me."

"I'm not that good-looking, but there are sure a lot of women out there who want a man, any man, and anybody's man. And then there are all those 'friends' who would like to set me up with a date. I'm a married man, but it doesn't make any difference to them." But John was a Christian and he waited and prayed. One day we got a phone call, "We're back together" he fairly shouted. Unconditional love works.

We heard a friend make a statement one day that literally made us gasp. He was a Christian man with a large ministry when the unthinkable happened, he became involved with another woman. We told him he had no other option but to stay with his wife and make his marriage work. He angerly declared, "I would rather go to hell." But he didn't, because God in his mercy turned him around AND healed his marriage.

We felt so sorry for Joyce, who would call several times a week just to hear, "You're going to make it". One day Dana told her, "Call me back tomorrow. I'm getting too sympathetic."

She told us several years later that Dana must have told her at least 500 times, "Sympathy kills, compassion gives life." You really hurt with the ones going through the trauma of a threatened divorce.

Her husband, Jim had been a leader in the charismatic movement. He had been a soul winner. But he sympathized with a lady who was having marital problems, and soon became involved. He became so involved that he left his wife and children. He moved in with the woman he had been counseling to try and save her marriage. He never stopped ministering in churches. He believed he could have God's anointing while living in adultery.

Joyce was broken-hearted, but never gave up believing God was going to turn him around and bring him home. She knew, that she knew, that she knew, God had heard her prayers and her marriage was healed. Jim became ill and nearly died, but God in his mercy saved his life, turned him around, and healed their marriage. Today, Jim is serving God as an ordained minister, and he and his wife are in the Marriage Healing Ministry.

God does bring beauty from ashes.

One day we received a phone call from a couple asking if they could stop by on their honeymoon. Of course they could! We were thrilled!

We had been standing with Ann for 8 years. Her husband had divorced her and married another woman with whom he had several children. Ann and her children had been waiting for Daddy to come home, even though this is not a popular stand. But, God's Word does say, I will make them one flesh, and they will never again be two. So she waited and prayed.

One night she received a phone call from her husband Bill, asking if he could come visit her and the children. His second wife had left him, and one day as he was watching "700 Club" he recommitted his life to Christ. When he called them, they advised him to seek God's guidance. The more he read the Word and prayed, the more he became convinced that Ann was the wife of his youth and his only wife.

When Bill visited Ann and the children, he got down on his knees and asked her to remarry him. She was ecstatic when she called us that same evening to tell us the news. They were remarried by a justice of the peace, because as Bill declared, "The state took us apart, the state can put us back together." And together they are. Bill's children from his second marriage visit them regularly.

One of the most dramatic stories of unconditional love was told to us by a pastor in Texas about his good friend, Jim who was a very active leader in the church. He asked Jim one day, "Have you always been a Christian?" Jim laughed and said, "Oh, no, I was a heathen. I drank and I ran around. I wouldn't have anything to do with God. My wife was a Christian and I really gave her a rough time. I wanted none of that religious stuff."

"My wife loved the Lord and attended church every Sunday. I stayed home every Sunday. I told her she could go to church, but just make SURE my dinner was ready on time. My wife would get dinner ready before she would leave for church and then give me a kiss and ask 'Would you like to go to church with me?'"

"One particular Sunday, I was in a very bad mood. My wife had just poured a cup of scalding hot coffee for me. As she was leaving, she asked the same question, 'Would you like to go to church with me today?' I exploded and screamed at her, throwing the cup of scalding coffee in her face. She calmly walked into the other room, washed, changed her clothes, and as she went out the door, she called out, 'Good-bye, honey, I'm leaving. I'll see you when I get home.'"

"The Holy Spirit convicted me and I was miserable. So miserable, I couldn't stay home. So, I followed my wife to church. When I walked in the door, I saw her down at the altar praying for me. It was too much. I literally ran down to the altar, gave my life to Jesus, and I have been serving Him ever since. I couldn't get away from my wife's unconditional love."

Many of you have heard of the famous preacher, Smith Wigglesworth. The story is told that one day he and his wife had a big fight. (this was before his conversion). He was so furious with her that even though it was nighttime, he locked her out of the house. She spent the night sleeping on their doorstep.

The next morning when he unlocked the door, she literally fell in the door onto the kitchen floor. She jumped up, shook herself off, and cheerfully asked, "And, what would you like to have for breakfast, Smith?"

She was quite a woman. And, Smith became quite a man.

A common thread goes through the healed marriages. The thread in unconditional love. You first surrender yourself to God, then surrender your mate to God, and then you love them with the love that Jesus loves.

No accusations, No ultimatums, No threats, No demands! You just love them and EXPECT God to bring them home because:

LOVE NEVER FAILS

Chapter 7

Never Give Up!

*W*hat is the secret ingredient to winning? The answer is never quitting. Quitting is never an option to a winner. You just REFUSE to give up. The ONLY way you can lose is to quit.

Winston Churchill was a winner. During World War II, Hitler had conquered Holland in less than a week and ALL the experts believed England was next on the list. Without the leadership of Winston Churchill, England would have been the next conquest. But, Mr. Churchill refused to be conquered.

He gave the shortest Commencement address in history when he spoke to the graduates at Harrow School on October 29, 1941. His charge to them was: "NEVER GIVE IN, NEVER GIVE IN, NEVER, NEVER, NEVER, NEVER." Churchill lived by this motto, refused defeat, and England was saved.

Terry Anderson refused to give up hope that some-day he would be a free man. He was held captive longer than any other hostage. Imagine being chained and blindfolded for months. When interviewed on T.V., he was asked how he was able to cope with the loneliness of months of solitary confinement. He instantly answered, "I EMBRACED the loneliness."

What a marvelous lesson we can learn from Terry. Don't fight the loneliness, embrace it, and never give up hope. Our entire nation rejoiced when we heard the news that Terry was coming home.

In Mrs. Cowman's devotional book, *Streams in the Desert*, V. 2 February 26, she states, "Sorrows are too precious to be wasted. They are God's winds that take our life and lift it to higher levels." Don't waste your sorrow, God is lifting you to a higher level. You will became a better person because of it. When you go through the valley of weeping, dig a well!

Dennis Byrd, who was paralyzed in a football injury, refused to quit. He determined, "I will walk out of this hospital." The Doctors said, "I hope so." Dennis said, "I know so." The Doctor stated as he watched Dennis WALK up to the platform to speak, "I wish I knew the secret ingredient Dennis has." The secret ingredient Dennis has is the determination to Never give up, and just plain, Never quit.

Dan Jansen refused to give up his quest for the gold medal in the Olympics of 1994. He just reached down deep inside himself and resolved he would not be denied the gold medal. Our entire nation rejoiced with him as he skated his victory skate holding his baby daughter.

One of my favorite stories is the story of Norman Williams. We have been privileged to hear him give this testimony several times. Norman was a passenger on one of the airplanes that was involved in the tragedy in the Canary Islands several years ago. An airplane had attempted to take off and crashed right on top of his plane. Both planes were an instant inferno.

Norman looked around and saw everybody around him literally being burned alive, and as he said, melting down before his very eyes. He remembered his Mother's prayer for his safety just before he left on the trip. He walked up the aisle of the airplane through walls of flames, held his hands up, praised the Lord, and declared, "I will **not** believe my circumstances, I **will** believe God's Word in Isaiah 43:2 which says, "When thou walkest through the fire thou shalt not be burned, neither shall the flames kindle upon thee."

Norman looked up, saw a hole in the ceiling of the plane, climbed up and out (he doesn't have the vaguest idea how) and jumped off the wing just seconds before the plane exploded. God supernaturally spared him and to make sure everyone knew it was God who performed the miracle, HE took the smell of smoke away from Norman's clothes. Hundreds died in this crash and the only reason Norman Williams didn't die is that he believed God's Word instead of his circumstances.

In contrast, the story is told of a swimmer who tried to swim from Catalina island to the mainland. She had been swimming for hours with no land in sight. The people in the support boat kept encouraging her, telling her she could make it. It was extremely foggy and she begged her crew to take her out of the water. They kept encouraging her, "Just a little further, just a little further." Finally, she gave up and the crew reluctantly lifted her into their boat.

Immediately the fog lifted. Imagine her dismay when she was lifted into the boat and saw land just one half mile away. **She could have made it.** She said afterwards, "I was not defeated by the cold or fatigue, but by not being able to see my goal." She had been just yards away from realizing her dream. If only she hadn't given up.

How sad it is when we give up just yards short of realizing our dream. We don't know when we will see our dream fulfilled. We just must never give up, never give up, never give up.

Ephesians 6:13 tells us, "Having done all to stand, STAND!!!!! We not only have seen marriages come back together after divorce, remarriage, divorce from the second mate and then remarriage to original mate, but we have seen divorce, remarriage, divorce, remarriage, divorce, and remarriage to original mate after 20 years. Prodigals do come home, believe it or not.

God is not in the marriage-breaking-up business. HE is in the marriage restoration business. God is also in the miracle business. We received two baby announcements, both from couples who had reconciled. One had been married almost 20 years and had their first baby. The other couple had been married 13 years and had their first baby. Isn't God wonderful?

There are multitudes of pastors, counselors, friends and family who will sympathize with your hurt. They will advise you that if your mate has been gone any length of time, (this could be one month or one year) that your marriage is dead...dead...dead... dead.

This is what "Job's friends" usually tell you. "God doesn't want you to hurt. God wants you to be happy." Or they will advise you, "This has gone on long enough. Get on with your life." The postscript is usually, "God has someone better for you."

Those famous three phrases have brought death and destruction to many, many marriages. We have heard them hundreds of times from standers calling in. They say, "This is what EVERYBODY tells us. We say, "But it isn't what God's Word tells you." The bottom line is God says HE made you one flesh, and you will never again be two.

When you realize that the scripture is really true when it says in II Corinthians 4:4 that "Satan, who is the god of the evil world has made him blind," you don't take things that your mate does to you personally. When Dana would say to me, "I can't stand to be in the same room with you," I would joyfully tell the Lord, "Thank you that Dana loves me so much." I refused to take personally any words that hurt. After all the deceived are deceived.

Isaiah 44:20 says "He feeds on ashes. A deluded heart misleads him. He cannot save himself or say, is not this thing in my right hand a lie." Then you apply Job 5:8. "But if I were you, I would appeal to God. I would lay my cause before Him. He performs wonders that cannot be fathomed, miracles that cannot be counted."

"Wine, women, and song make a man lose his brains." Hosea 4:11. One well-known singer who was fantasizing about another woman later confessed to his wife, "It was like my brain was under anesthetic."

A pastor stated, "Sin is insane." After 40 years of a wonderful marriage, he had become involved with another woman. Both of these storys had a happy ending because their wives stood and would not give up no matter how hopeless it looked.

The saddest story I ever heard was told by a man who was being interviewed on a Christian radio program. "My wife got so tired of waiting for me to straighten up, that she divorced me and married someone else. Now I am a Christian and living for the Lord." Choking up with tears he added, "If only she had waited a little longer we would still be together."

When you decide that no matter what, you are never going to give up on your marriage, it's like signing up for the service during a war. You are in it for the duration. The duration may be six weeks, six years, or sixteen years. You just have no other option if you want to forgive the way Jesus forgives. Job 22:30 tells us that "Though he is not innocent, he will be saved through the cleanness of your hands."

But, how do you get to the place that you refuse to give up on your marriage? You make a quality decision there will be no turning back. You have passed the point of return. Now you have no other option but to stand for your marriage to be healed. As the British Naval Captain ordered as he faced his enemy's ship, "Nail that flag to the mast. There will be NO Surrender."

A husband sat and sobbed, his head in his hands.

He looked at his wife, who had been faithfully waiting for him to come home while he had affair after affair with other women.

"All of my friends have been having affairs. And when they do, their wives start having affairs too for revenge. I am so thankful you never stepped out on me even though I deserved it," he chokingly told her between sobs. She told us she looked in his eyes and could see that he had made the change from the kingdom of darkness to the kingdom of light. She had waited 10 years to hear this. Was it worth it? What is a man's soul worth? She was ecstatic.

We have all seen ball games where someone was way behind and it appeared there was absolutely no way they could win the game. But, because they would not quit and they refused to give up, they came from behind and won the victory. As the saying goes, "It's never over until it's over."

Some of you may be saying, "My marriage is over. He has been gone for __ years, and is never coming home." Never, Never, Never, Never give up.

A friend had called me when we were going through the deepest valley and said, "I have a scripture from the Lord for you today." HE says, "Stand Back and see the incredible rescue operation I am going to do for you." The day my marriage was healed was an incredible rescue operation. There was no explanation except God will be God.

God never, never, never, never gave up on our marriage and He will never, never, never, never give up on yours.

When we were in Oregon for a Marriage Seminar, someone handed me A Stander's Affirmation. I thought it was excellent and I would like to share it with you. It was written by Pastor Bob Moorehead, Overlake Christian Church, Kirkland, Washington.

A STANDER'S AFFIRMATION

I AM STANDING FOR THE HEALING OF MY MARRIAGE!...I will not give up, give in, give out or give over 'till that healing takes place. I made a vow, I said the words, I gave the pledge, I gave a ring, I took a ring, I gave myself, I trusted God, and said the words, and meant the words...in sickness and in health, in sorrow and in joy, for better or for worse, for richer or for poorer, in good times and in bad..., so I am standing NOW, and will not SIT down, LET down, SLOW down, CALM down, FALL down, LOOK down, or be DOWN 'til the breakdown is TORN down!

I refuse to put my eyes on outward circumstances, or listen to prophets of doom, or buy into what is trendy, worldly, popular, convenient, easy, quick, thrifty, or advantageous.. nor will I settle for a cheap imitation of God's real thing, nor will I seek to lower God's standard, twist God's will, re-write God's Word, violate God's covenant, or accept what God hates, namely divorce!!!

In a world of filth, I will stay pure; surrounded by lies, I will speak the truth; where hopelessness abounds, I will hope in God: where revenge is easier, I will bless instead of curse; and where the odds are stacked against me, I will trust in God's faithfulness.

I am a STANDER, and I will not acquiesce, compromise, quarrel or quit...I have made the choice, set my face, entered the race, believed the Word, and trusted God for all the outcome.

I will allow neither the reaction of my spouse, nor the urging of my friends, nor the advice of my loved ones, nor economic hardship, nor the prompting of the devil to make me let up, slow up, blow up, or give up 'til my marriage is healed!!!!!![1]

NEVER, NEVER, NEVER, NEVER GIVE UP...HOPE

---

[1] Used by permission of Bob Moorehead

Chapter 8

~⊷⊷∞⊷⊷~

Olga

$\mathcal{W}$ e first met Olga at one of our seminars in Ohio. She had gotten our name and phone number, from a counselor at the "700 Club" and had called us. We talked to her on the phone many times and finally met her in person at the seminar. We were impressed with her sincerity, and with her love for Jesus. She had black snappy eyes and laughter that was contagious.

Olga called regularly over a period of five or six years. We would pray with her and encourage her to stand for her marriage, even though her husband, Ismael was living in Texas with another woman. I remember the day she called and cried, "The divorce is supposed to be final today." But God had other plans. Instead of the divorce being final that day, Ismael came home to his wife that day.

Olga still called us after Ismael returned home. She found out that just because your mate comes home, it doesn't mean all your problems are suddenly over. But, then we got the phone call that thrilled us beyond words to describe. "Ismael and I want to come to your church and give our testimony about how God healed our marriage," Olga joyfully announced. They came and we had the service taped. We knew thousands of standers would identify with Olga's testimony, so I had it printed as a brochure and it has gone out all over the United States.

We were blessed to attend Ismael's ordination. It wasn't long until they felt called to quit their jobs, sell everything, get in their car, and head for Texas and Mexico. They knew God had called them to minister to broken marriages. Since they were ministering to a lot of Spanish-speaking people, we had Olga and Ismael's testimony translated into Spanish as well as English.

Here is their testimony. We pray it will bring New Hope to your Broken Marriage.

THIRD TIME YOU'RE OUT! Olga didn't think so. The third time she received divorce papers from her husband she....Well, I'll let her tell the story.

"We will be married 27 years this November (1993) and God has done a tremendous work in our marriage. August 10, 1987, my husband filed for divorce for the third time. Here I had been interceding for our marriage, and believing that God was going to bring my husband home. Getting those papers was like tearing my flesh in two. All the old wounds were open again.

All I wanted to do was to go to my best-friend and cry on her shoulder, but the Holy Spirit said NO, go to your room and pray. So I obeyed and went to my room and knelt down. The Lord gave me a scripture I will never forget. It is in Isaiah 66:13 — "For I shall comfort you as a Mother comforts a child." He knew my hurt, He knew how badly I was hurting, but He was there to comfort me."

"God turned the impossible around in my life. A lot of people told me to give up, that Ismael wasn't worth it. But, God told me differently. And I thank God for those who lifted me up when I needed a word of encouragement. I praise God for those who stood with me when there was no hope."

"Three times he sent me the divorce papers, but he

never once went through with the divorce. The Lord was always working in his life and I would tell the Lord, 'Don't let him forget the calling you have put on his life, and no matter where he is, reach him, Lord. Send your ministering angels to him and give him no peace until he comes back to you.' God has done it and every time I see him behind the pulpit, I cry because I see what God has done in Ismael's life when the enemy had tried to destroy him."

"My home was a wreck. My children didn't want anything to do with their father. They wouldn't even talk to him. I felt like I was between two tall walls. But God had given me scripture that He was going to bring Ismael back from the land of the enemy and my children would return back from the land of the border. He told me there was Hope in my future. I believed God, not what I saw with my eyes."

"There were a lot of people who tried to discourage me by telling me my husband wasn't worth it and God had someone better for me, but God would tell me differently."

"It was a lot harder to intercede for my husband after he returned home. When he was gone I would always set a plate for him at the table, with a cup of coffee and a glass of water. With my spiritual eyes I would see him there. I would leave and when I would come back inside my apartment, I would call out 'Hi, Honey, I'm home', even though he wasn't there to hear me. But, by faith I saw him there."

"I thank God for the people God uses when we need help. Sometimes we just need lifting up. I thank God for having those people in my life, and for people like Don and Fran Brunner who have Dana and Val's tape ministry and have copied all their tapes."

"As I said before, my marriage was a disaster, my children would have nothing to do with their Dad. But, I thank God that He broke the yoke and we're a family again. We're closer as a family than we have ever been, and I praise Jesus for that."

Ismael, Olga's husband interjects, "I thank God for being here tonight at New Hope Church and like my wife was saying, thanks to everyone who interceded for me while I was gone. God kept me alive for a reason and He's the reason I'm alive. God had called me when I was a young man and instead of doing the work of God, I was doing the work of the devil. It would hurt when people who knew I had been a preacher would say to me, 'What are you doing in a place like this?'"

"God protected me when I was in danger of losing my life more than 3 or 4 times. God had His hand on me and I knew why. I knew there was a beautiful lady who never got tired of praying for me. I thank God for giving me a wonderful wife who had an unconditional love that would not let her do anything but love me, even though I kept hurting her.

I thank God Olga never gave up, even though I kept on doing the bad things to her after I came back. I was down in prison in sin. The devil had taken me the lowest a man can go. I even started dealing drugs, and used them myself...me a preacher. He took care of me, or I would be dead today. Now every day I tell God, 'Take me as the potter takes the clay, and make my life what You want it to be. Use me, and send me where You want to send me.'"

"Now, there's nothing I can do to thank God enough for all He has done for me. I thank God for this wonderful wife He has given me and for healing the deep wounds that were in her heart. There's nobody else that can heal those kind of wounds, Only God. He's the healer, not only of the body, but of the soul. It was her love, her unconditional love that she showed me, even though I kept hurting her, that brought me back home."

When asked, what stopped the divorce from going through the third time, Olga replied, "Ismael had gone back to Texas to marry the other woman, but when he went back, the Lord changed his plans. She had somebody else. So, the day the divorce was to be final, Ismael came home and the divorce was stopped by default."

Olga goes on. "Like I said, three times I got divorce papers in the mail. The last time I went into my bedroom and prayed on my knees. I got up, and addressed the devil. `Devil, you're not going to win.' I said, "I'm going to church and I am getting a blessing from the Lord.

That night I came home and went into my room. I opened my Bible and the Lord gave me the scripture in Jeremiah 31:16,17 which says "Refrain your voice from weeping and your eyes from tears, for I shall reward your works and he shall return back from the land of the enemy, and there is hope for you, and thy children shall return back from the land of the border." (Olga's translation)

"That night I didn't sleep. I danced and I shouted in the spirit. I was so excited that God had given me that scripture. And all the scriptures God has given me have been fulfilled in my life."

"He also gave me Habakuk 2:3, that says wait on the vision. Sometimes we get so discouraged, we want to help the Lord and God doesn't need our help. We don't need to do what we think God isn't getting done."

"That's where we make a mistake. God was telling me to wait. After Ismael came back, he would do all these hurtful things like not coming home until 4 or 5 in the morning. I wanted to give up and tell him how I hurt, but the Lord wouldn't let me. All I could do was just love him. I even got to the point I wanted to tell him to leave...I couldn't stand the hurt. But, again the Lord wouldn't allow me to do this."

"The Holy Spirit spoke to me one day and said, 'I have given you so many scriptures of hope, and if you tell Ismael to leave, he is going to be lost forever. In the day of judgment, I will hold you accountable for his soul.' "Oh, I don't want that," I cried. "I will continue to pray and stand for my marriage and for my husband's salvation. I will let God work it out."

"Even when we got back together Ismael didn't want me to ask him to go to church. So I went by myself. I never pushed him to go. (I Peter 3:1 says in the Living, "Wives, fit in with your husband's plans, for then if they refuse to listen when you talk to them about the Lord, they will be won by your respectful, pure behavior.") So, I decided I was going to win him to the Lord without saying a word."

"One of my relatives told me what I needed was a psychiatrist because she would see my husband come and leave and come and leave. She thought I was crazy for not telling him to leave permanently. I told her I had a psychiatrist, the best there is, Jesus."

"I thank God, that even though I went through a lot, getting divorce papers three times, God shaped every circumstance for my good. The Lord wanted to take things from my life. One thing was pride. I had a lot of pride. I thank God that going through everything helped me to grow in my spiritual life. I know God has a purpose for everything that happens in our lives. What Satan meant for our harm, God turned around for our good."

"I thank God He gave me the strength to hold on and not give up, to stand firm in His Word. The Word says to cast all your cares upon Him, for He careth for you, and so I just cast my husband upon Him, and then the Lord started working in his life."

"Ismael would tell me that when he was in Texas, there would be times he couldn't sleep and he would dream of me and dream of the kids and would be very miserable. I said, well, thank you Lord for that, because that's the way I wanted him to feel."

"When he would call from Texas, I would say, 'I love

you', but he would never reply. I don't understand the love the Lord gave me for him myself. I had never experienced this kind of love before in my life.

One night the Lord gave me a dream. I was seeing beautiful waters and there was like a light, but I couldn't see His face but it was shiny. HE would tell me to cross the water to him, but I would say 'I'm afraid, I can't swim.' But HE said, 'Come on,' so I did. When I got to him, it was Jesus and HE said, 'Go back, now , it's going to be alright.'"

"The next day I went to a prayer meeting and a lady whom I had never seen before started giving me scripture and she told me that from this day forth you will never be the same. The Lord has answered your prayers. And all my prayers were answered."

"There aren't enough words to thank the Lord for what He has done in our lives. No human doctor could have healed our wounds. We were shattered in a thousand pieces. No doctor could have healed our children's wounds. But God did!!!"

"God is a God of miracles. On July 31, 1993, my husband was ordained as a minister of the gospel. Only God could have taken ashes and made beauty."

"PRAISE HIS NAME FOREVER."

Chapter 9

The Val and Dana Tape

*W*hen people started calling us after our marriage was healed, we had no intention of ever making a tape to help them. But, Dana said one Sunday evening in church, "Let's share with our congregation what we are telling people who call us."

Fran taped the service and the rest is history. We have sent out thousands of the Val and Dana tape to hurting people. Many people have told us that they have listened to the tape until they have worn it out. They ask, "Would you please send me another Val and Dana tape? I about have it memorized, but I still need another one."

When we made this tape, we had just started in this ministry. We listened to it ourselves in total disbelief. We couldn't believe how unprofessional it sounded. We hesitated with long pauses while we searched for scripture. We even discussed whether we wanted to send the tape out or not.

But God anointed our stumblings and bumblings, when we didn't have the knowledge of the Word that we have now. We praise God it has been an encouragement to so many people.

People have to have hope and we pray this chapter will give New Hope to you as you read it. Dana begins the conversation.

"If ever there is a time that it is true, that you MUST stick with the WORD. it is when you are dealing with a marriage. Stay With The Word!!!"

"In opening I want to share two scriptures with you that give a basis that we have to work from. One is from Malachi 2:14, 'Yet you say for what reason, because the Lord has been witness between you and the wife of your youth, with whom you have dealt treacherously: yet is she thy companion, (and note this last phrase) she is your wife *by covenant.'* "She is not your wife because you went up to the courthouse and got a license, and got married."

"Proverbs 2:17 tells of the woman, who has left the partner of her youth and ignored the covenant she made before God. So this covenant goes both ways. Val usually gets the calls, so go on ahead and share what you usually share with the callers."

"Some of them call and say, 'There's another woman'. I say, Another woman is not the problem. The scripture is Ephesians 6:12. We wrestle not against flesh and blood, but against principalities and powers. And so if your mate is flesh and blood, they are not the problem."

"Realize what she is saying. Anything that touches the five senses is not the problem. And your mate fits that category, because he or she is flesh and blood. You talk to a lady and her husband has a couple of girl friends, and you tell her they are not the problem, she thinks you're flaky."

"I repeat it at least five times."

"It just goes over her head. She is so SURE that gal is her problem that it just goes right by her."

"One of the first things I tell them, (I think Sue coined this phrase), is that God is not in the marriage breaking-up business. God hates divorce. So, you can pray knowing that God will hear you because it is His Will to save your marriage. You don't have to ask Him if it is His

Will to heal your marriage."

"Again, anchor it in The Word. Malachi 2:16. God hates divorce."

"We're studying in James now, and in James 3:16 it says, 'For where envying and strife is there is confusion and every evil work.' So ladies, if there is any strife in your house, you have opened your house up for every evil work. So, what I usually talk to them about is how to get the strife out of their home. For one thing, you can take authority over it. It's a spirit. I take authority over the strife in this house in the name of Jesus, and I command it to leave. You may have to do this several times a day."

"We want to establish one thing first of all. One of the ladies we are standing with asked, 'Since my husband has been gone over a year, should I have any physical relationship with him? (He had been coming home some) Is this almost adultery?'"

"He's your husband."

"Anything you do to establish a division, recognizes a division. You have to realize that if you are claiming a marriage, you have to act married. If you're married, you're married."

"Every man and every woman has to have a haven. Do you know what a haven is? That's a place where you can go and hide from the world. And all your problems and all your difficulties don't matter. You've got a place where you can go and shut the world outside. He has to know there is a place where he can go and not be threatened and criticized. When you establish that haven, then you begin to realize what we're talking about in relation to strife. You never EVER talk about the problem in terms of the flesh. The flesh will say, 'Talk about the problem, talk about him drinking too much, talk about the fact he has a girl friend.'"

"Men leave for different reasons as women leave for different reasons. But, it doesn't change the pattern. So the fleshly reason this division has come is really not important, because we wrestle not against flesh and blood. When you're establishing a haven, the last thing you need to have happen is to have the 'innocent party' start questioning you about what happened."

"I'll never forget one time we were on our way to Ludington for a business appointment. Val was with me and on the way up things were good. The healing was in process and it was a beautiful time. But, we learned that healing is 5 years down the road. You don't discuss things. Just because the blood quits running, doesn't mean you are healed. It means it's scabbed over, and when you knock the scab off, it's harder to heal. Val and I got into an innocent discussion and by the time we got to Ludington, the warfare was full blown."

"Ladies, do you realize that women are 80% more manipulative than men? I heard that at a Full Gospel meeting with General Schaeffer's wife. And I hate to admit this, but one time when we were counseling with a lady, (have you ever talked to somebody and all of a sudden seen yourself?), I got hot and cold and hot and cold. I said, that's me and I quit talking. As we were talking to this lady, she was telling us that her husband just treated her wonderful, like a queen, for the first 20 years of their married life. Then things cooled off."

"Dana asked her, 'Do you always have a better way of doing things? Do you tell him how to do everything?' She was always second guessing him. When she said, 'Yes, that was a problem with her,' I realized that second-guessing was my problem too. Just to go to town, I had a better way to go. The most divisive thing that ever came into our marriage was me having to second guess Dana and having a better way of doing everything. And Ladies, that's a characteristic of women and we have to get rid of it."

"When we were first married, an opportunity came up to buy a farm that I was just desperate to take. But

Val wouldn't even go look at it. This year on our vacation, I took her by the place. We had an awful time finding it because it was an abandoned farm. I know now, I never could have made it with a wife and four kids, but we would have been ahead to have gone there and gone bankrupt, because I would have learned responsibility."

"As long as a man can put the blame for his failures on a wife who says, 'Don't do this, do this', as soon as you do that, Ladies, you take the responsibility, and you are going to get it in the neck. Everything that went wrong from that point on was Val's fault in my eyes, because she wouldn't let me do what I felt to do. I would have matured then instead of 30 years later."

"What we women are saying is, We can't trust the Lord to take care of our husbands. We women have to do it. Have any of you read Leilani Watt's book? She's James Watt's wife. It is terrific. Their marriage was horrible. He was a very domineering man and kinda pounded her down until she was a nobody. And the Lord told her, HER job in Washington D.C. was to intercede for her husband. So every morning, with no interruptions, she interceded for her husband. One morning the Lord gave her a Word,'Get in your husband's boat' She said,'What???' "

"The Lord said, you are in your own boat. The Lord gave her a vision of two boats out there, one tied with a rope to the other. And she can kind of go where she pleases, although she is tied to the other boat. She can come close, or go in the opposite direction, but she wasn't really with him. So, she got in his boat. All that changed was her attitude."

"I would say in most marriages the partners are in two boats. They need to get in the same boat. You have to do it."

"Criticism and strife you have to counsel out of a home, if it is going to come back together."

"It gets to be a habit. Husbands and wives will cut each other down. But, I learned something last week and this has been the happiest week of our life. I found something to praise Dana about every day, sometimes twice a day. And it's the Word. In Ephesians it says the husband must love his wife as he loves himself, and the wife must respect, or reverence her husband. So, I have been praising Dana every day and Dana has been telling me he loves me every day."

"This came out of what Bob Trench said last Sunday when he said, 'A man needs to have his ego pumped up and a woman needs to be loved.' We have been taught for years that ego is a problem. Ego is what makes a man a man, and what makes him the head of his house. When a man is lifted up, he does not doubt himself."

Most of us have so much rejection. This is what I fought as a young man growing up, rejection, rejection, rejection. Constantly striving, but never able to achieve. But, when the rejection was turned off and the building up began, Man, that's a heady experience.

"A man who has his ego where it ought to be can love himself, and Ladies, I want to tell you something, no man can love you unless he loves himself. What comes from man who does not love himself is lust, because he wants You to make him something."

"I want to go to some of the don'ts. NEVER say the word, divorce. Never let it cross your mouth. It's not an option, it's not even a topic of discussion. It starts a chain reaction, and pretty soon you're getting a divorce, even though you never intended to get a divorce. But, it gave you an option. But, there is no option."

"Whatever you put in your mind, will come out when you least expect it. Whatever you feed, grows. Whatever you feed in comes out. If he has a girlfriend, or she has a boyfriend, you never mention the name. You refuse to recognize the existence of the situation. Are you putting your head in the sand? No, you are calling those things that are not as though they are. For after all, a third party is not the problem."

"Another don't. Don't harangue. Don't nag. But harangue is more than nag, it is hanging on like a bull dog. You just keep going over it , and over it and over it."

"Another thing that is a problem is when husbands and wives get into a fight, they bring up everything that has happened in the last 10 years. It's against the family law to bring up anything that's over 12 hours old. Just don't do it."

"Almost always, the finances have gone down the tube when the couple is having problems. Their mind has gone tilt."

"Normally, this is the case, that money and the handling of money creates a desire to handle it without being curtailed. So, when a person is not accustomed to handling money and they take authority in money situations, shipwreck is about to happen. Not because they are ignorant, but because they just don't know how to handle it.

"When there is a problem like this, it must be recognized that there is an illness. We're talking about sin-sickness. I share this from where I was. A dear pastor came and talked to me and I agreed with everything he said. He said all the right things, but it meant different things to him than it did to me. What I perceived he said was not what he said.

"And so we counsel a wife when your husband has gone tilt, you don't believe anything he says and you don't take anything personally. He is acting perfectly natural for someone controlled by Satan. He has a problem, don't make it yours. You don't treat that person as though he could think rationally. Their mind is simply tilted, and their thinking is different than yours.

"No woman would leave a man who is dying of cancer. And when this kind of thing happens, the individual that has gone away emotionally is literally dying spiritually, and in many ways physically. So, you stay and nurse them through. You just don't quit. You refuse to give up."

"I prayed for a supernatural love for Dana when we went through our problems, and God gave it to me. He could say anything to me, and I wouldn't take it personally. I'd say 'Thank you Father, for my husband who loves me so much. Thank you, Father, that my marriage is healed.' I said this over and over and over again."

"Prayer is our lethal weapon. But, it is difficult to tell people who are standing on the edge of a precipice to put their confidence in something they can't see."

"Faith prays, 'Thank you for my husband who is so considerate of me, thank you that my husband loves the Word of God so much, thank you my husband is so gentle and kind', and he may be hitting you over the head. But, you get what you say. If you say my husband is so mean to me, that's what you get."

"You have to sell out to the fact that your marriage is healed, or even though you say the right words to your mate, it will come across as the wrong words. Your commitment is not based on your circumstances, your commitment is based on the Word and the covenant commitment that you have with God."

"One lady told me, don't get out of bed until you plead the blood of Jesus over Dana. So, I would do this while he was still asleep. Another thing I did was anoint everything in the house, every window, every door, all the furniture, the car. A handkerchief that had been anointed at a Full Gospel Meeting for Dana would make him violent every time I would put it under his pillow. I don't know how many times I would take it out and put it back under his pillow."

"Paul says, bring the prayer cloth and have it anointed. There is power in this."

"Always act like you are married. You keep your wedding rings on. If you want your marriage to come back together, act like it's coming back together."

"A friend of our daughter, Jayne, wanted to get married, but had not even met her future husband, so she made a wedding dress. She got married. If a person has left the home and happens to come back at meal time and there are three places set, and there are four in the family, the message, loud and clear, is that you are not a part of this home. There ought not be a table set without a plate and even a glass of water for the mate who left. In other words you walk every step of the way as though your marriage is healed."

"Another thing is, don't counsel with numerous people. Only counsel with those who believe sincerely that you are going to make it. We had this one lady who was counseling with several spirit-filled Christians. They were telling her, go ahead, make your own life, get on with your life, get a divorce. Thank goodness she didn't listen to them and her marriage is within inches of being healed."

"I praise God that when we went through the valley, Val never spoke to other people about the problem. If you love that mate and want them to come back, you want everybody to be a supporter of them. I told one lady as she was telling me all the garbage about how her husband was treating her, remember one thing, you are really hurting, but remember you are not hurting as bad as he hurt, because he hurt so bad he ran."

"This one lady calls me often and apologizes for calling. I say, 'No, it's a privilege.' It's just been lately after 5 years, that Dana and I can say, Praise you that we went through the valley, because now we can help others go through what we went through. God gave me Bible verses all through that time. One of the verses I really hung on to was, 'I will perfect that which concerns you' so, the time he had the shotgun and said I'm going to go kill myself and I'll kill you if you try and stop me. I said, If you have to, you have to.'"

"Really makes you feel important."

"I had the confidence that God had said he was going to perfect that which concerned me. I didn't have a doubt in the world that he was NOT going to kill himself even though he had the shotgun and two shells and had taken off in the car. I knew, that I knew, that I knew that God was going to perfect that which concerneth me."

"Do you realize what she is saying here? It is authority. Her confidence in the Lord gave her authority over the situation and there wasn't anything I could do about it, because I didn't have that authority."

Do any of you have any questions?

A lady from the audience asked if we knew what the word harangue means?

Dana asked her, What's your definition?

She answered, "It's a combination word of harass and nag."

We asked, "How many times do you hear a wife say "My husband nagged me to death?""

"Not too often, it's usually the wife who nags her husband to death, because we're manipulative and our husband doesn't do what we want him to do when we want him to do it, so we start nagging. We don't trust the Lord to get it done, and how important is it anyhow? Not too, when you consider your marriage may be at stake."

"Maybe you ladies have a pretty good idea of how things ought to be done, but that's not really important. A lady whose husband is struggling over this thing of a better idea, if she can just grasp that her greatest privilege is to live in the aura of a Christ like love from a husband. Wow, wouldn't you like to. He is obligated for every need you have. Husbands, apply that to you and you have the obligation to supply every need of your wife, in every area of her life. So, it's not a bad thing, ERA not withstanding."

"Another thing is, you have to release your husband or wife to the Lord. Let the Lord have the responsibility for bringing your mate home. Don't you try and talk him home. He won't listen. We're not in the people changing business, God is!!"

"Women ask should I quote the Bible to him and show him where he is wrong? NO! I Peter 3:1 says the wife will win the husband without the word by her behavior."

"We just came across this lately, about taking authority over the satanic thoughts in their mind. We're into a whole new ball game. You can't believe the people who have pornographic material in their homes. I would say about 90-95% of the people who call us have a problem with porno material in their homes. It is a spirit of lust which sometimes comes out ONLY by prayer and fasting."

"The hardest thing to get people to recognize is that they are the reason the other person left. That is really a toughie. The reason a person leaves, is that they are leaving something. At the same time, you have to not put yourself down, but love yourself. Don't take all the blame and say it's all my fault. But realistically, examine yourself, find out where you are and what needs changing?"

"Why is it that there is such a rending and tearing of flesh when one person leaves? Why is it that one person cries all the time? It's because the flesh is being torn in two."

One illustration I heard about why it hurts so badly is this: Take two pieces of say, typing paper. Completely cover them with super glue, put them together and leave them for how many years you have been married. Now try tearing them apart. You know what you get? Nothing but holes. That's why it hurts so badly. You are literally torn apart. I remember thinking, 'Will there ever be a day that I don't cry? I wondered, will I ever laugh again?'"

"Yeah, she laughs all the time."

"The easiest thing to tell someone would be to tell them, go ahead, get a divorce. That's the easy way. Because it's all up-hill work when you start standing for a marriage. I'm surprised someone didn't ask, 'Can every marriage be saved'?"

"Yep! Without exception. Father, we pray in a communing of Spirit with you tonight. You have blessed our home, and I thank you so much for the privilege of being a blessing to others who are hurting so much. Lord give understanding, and where maybe there is confusion over something that was said, you clarify it. You know Lord, that many times we say one thing, but it comes out something else. You make those adjustments that no home might know anything but blessing because of this night. And we'll give you the praise, and the honor and the glory for all that's accomplished. We pray that there will be many who will be able to praise Your Name because of tonight. In Jesus' Name, Amen."

**BIND US TOGETHER LORD,
WITH CORDS THAT CANNOT BE BROKEN
BIND US TOGETHER WITH LOVE**

Chapter 10

~⦿~

Hi Honey, I'm Home

"**H**I HONEY, I'M HOME!" Many of you have longed to hear those words for what seems like forever. It will be the happiest day of your life when your mate walks through the door and announces he or she is home to stay. FINALLY, your nightmare is over! So... so...don't blow it!

The words, home to stay, are the critical words in the paragraph above. If your husband or wife is typical of the ones we talk with, your emotions have been like a yo-yo for several months or even several years.

One minute your spouse tells you that he or she is coming home. The next minute they angrily declare they are NEVER coming home. When Dana and I went through this time in our lives, I would tell myself, "Well we went one step forward today, we'll probably go two steps backward tomorrow."

The wandering mate's goal seems to be to keep you guessing. They just don't want you to know when, or if, they are coming home. I have heard it called "The Recoil Theory." When they reach out to you and you think, "He or she is on their way home at last," they seem to pull-away, or recoil.

But, you just have to realize that this is part of the pattern of, "Today he hates me, tomorrow he loves me," and "Today he loves me, tomorrow he hates me." Don't get impatient, but wait for God to complete His work in your mate. When GOD brings him or her home they are home to stay.

Even though your husband or wife is now home, they are still very fragile and will be for some time...try several years, plus or minus. Our marriage had been healed five years before we attempted to help others.

At first, everything will be wonderful. After the "Honeymoon" though, you may be tempted to make them pay just a little for putting you through all that pain and agony while they were away. But, put away your smoking gun when you are tempted to react in wounding words. It is YOUR problem if your desire is to get a pound of flesh. The rule is, PRAY IT, DON'T SAY IT!!!!!

DON'T talk to them about what happened. DON'T let your curiosity bury you. Example: I've been wondering....I'd really like to know...if I could only understand what happened....You remember when....What was it like in the other world....Do you ever think about the other person...Have you ever contacted them...etc. etc. The rule of thumb is: "Don't say it! Pray it!!

When you see them staring into space with a far-away look in their eyes, don't assume they are thinking about the interlude and wishing they were someplace else. They may be agonizing before God, asking for forgiveness for what they have done to their family.

It doesn't matter how you couch the questions in a desire to heal or understand. The bottom line is, *You Don't Need All the Details to Forgive.* I need to know everything so I'll know how to pray is a NO, NO. Someplace in your walk, you learned to trust God to bring your mate home. Now, you have to trust God as you heal.

If you have truly given your spouse to God, it is God's responsibility to change them. It is your responsibility to surrender to God and let Him change you. And...quit trying to do what you think God isn't getting done. *The Battle Is the Lord's Not Yours.*

When you forgive, you cannot take any action on what you forgave, or you haven't forgiven. That is why divorce is the ultimate act of unforgiveness, and why divorce is so dangerous for a Christian. God's Word says just after the Lord's Prayer, that if you don't forgive, neither will God forgive you.

The following article, "Dying to Self" is a true test of whether you have died to self. Or, it's a test of whether you just MUST control every situation and regulate conditions. If you and your mate truly desire to become one-flesh, both must die to self. It is no longer what is best for me, but what is best for us.

Dying to Self

When you are forgotten, or neglected, or purposely set at naught, and you don't sting and hurt with the insult or the oversight, but your heart is happy, being counted worthy to suffer for Christ, That is Dying to Self.

When your good is evil spoken of, when your wishes are crossed, your advice disregarded, your opinions ridiculed, and you refuse to let anger rise in your heart, or even defend yourself, but take it all in patient, loving silence, That Is Dying to Self.

When you lovingly and patiently bear any disorder, and irregularity, and impunctuality, or any annoyance; when you can stand face to face with waste, folly, extravagance, spiritual insensibility...and endure it as Jesus endured it, That is Dying to Self.

When you are content with any food, any climate, any society, any solitude, any interruption by the will of God, That is Dying to Self.

When you never care to refer to yourself in conversation, or to record your own good works, or itch after commendation, when you can truly love to be unknown, That is Dying to Self.

When you can receive correction and reproof from one of less stature than yourself, and can humbly submit inwardly as well as outwardly, finding no rebellion or resentment rising up within your heart, That is Dying to Self.

In these last days, the Spirit would bring us to the Cross. "That I may know him...being made comformable to his death."

Author Unknown

When a man comes back home, a tough thing the woman has to deal with is, how to step down from being the spiritual head of the home. After all, she is the one who has spent hours in prayer and scripture reading. She has memorized scripture, fasted and prayed, trusted God and grown in leaps and bounds in her spiritual life. Her husband has been in sin, and just turned his life over to God. He is a baby Christian, and you can't expect a third grader to work calculus. Be patient! Pray and Trust God! God would rather do it Himself. Don't try and be the Holy Spirit to your mate.

A very difficult thing for the man to handle is his crushed ego when his wife has been unfaithful. It seems to be a lot easier for a woman to forgive adultery, than a man. But again, if he doesn't forgive her, neither will Christ forgive him. So he has no option, but to drive a stake and say, "Today, I forgive my wife." Here is an example of a man who did just that.

We almost always talk just to the mate who wants to save the marriage. But one day we got a phone call from a lady who asked "Can we come to your home?" I answered, "Sure, when would you like to come?" (it was quite a distance) " Tomorrow!" she quickly responded.

The husband had a doctorate in counseling, but it didn't help him with his unforgiveness for his wife of many years, who had committed adultery. He was tormented with thoughts of her being with another man. We talked with them for several hours with no break-through.

Finally Dana, who is very practical, suggested, "Why don't you go home, go into your backyard with a wooden stake and drive it into the ground. As you drive the stake down, forgive your wife for committing adultery. Then, when Satan comes with those tormenting thoughts, take him out to the stake in the back yard and tell him, `This is where I forgave her and there is the stake to prove it.'"

It didn't take too many trips to the backyard until the devil didn't bother to come around anymore with his accusations. His wife told us recently, "You can't believe what a marvelous marriage we have now."

Remember what we said on our first tape. Every day the wife needs to be told, "I love you.". And, every day the husband needs to hear what a wonderful man he is and that he is the most important person in your life.

At first you will be so thankful to have your mate home you will do this. But, as time goes one, there is a tendency to return to your old habit patterns.

Case in point. A lady I know lost 100 pounds in three years of agonizing effort, only to gain 120 pounds back in one year. Why? She returned to her old eating habits. So, when your mate returns home, don't revert back to the old "you".

Time after time people have told us, "I'm not the same person I was. I recognize how controlling I was, what a shrew I was, etc. etc. Or, in the case of the man, "I paid no attention to my wife's needs. All I did was watch sports on TV."

One lady called in a panic. Her husband had returned home after she had done an about-face in her life. She was one of the most controlling persons with whom I have ever talked. In fact, she got so angry at me one day when in frustration I blurted out "I can understand why your husband left you," that she slammed the receiver down.

She called back contrite, "You are right. I am a controlling person. With God's help, I will change." And when she did, her husband came home and they were as happy as newly-weds. But, after about six months she called and was very agitated about something her husband wanted to do.

After talking just a few minutes, I gently told her, "You are back to that person your husband couldn't stand. If he leaves again, there is only one person you can blame and that is YOU."

She began weeping and crying, "I am! I am! I'm my old self again." Her eyes were opened and she decided it was better to change herself once and for all, than to lose her husband. The last I heard from her, they were doing great.

Another big point of conflict when the marriage is healing is finance. Both are used to managing their own money. Now it is not my money, but our money. Couples miss a tremendous opportunity to express confidence in each other by not having a joint account. Preferring your spouse is the bottom line.

Remember your wedding vows? You promised in front of God and witnesses that you both gave each other ALL of your worldly goods. That was past, present and future.

You know the Number One reason for divorce is selfishness. We have a play-pen mentality with marriages. When two babies are in a play-pen and one takes a toy, you will soon hear a howl and a scream. Some people never seem to grow up. What is mine is mine, and what is yours is mine. It can't be this way in a marriage or the marriage will end in disaster. You must prefer each other.

What can you do after you're back together to improve your marriage? It is still a truth that the only person you can change is you. But, you still can praise God that He is making your mate into the person He planned for them to be.

Pray praise prayers. "I praise you my mate is so mature and treats me with such respect. I thank you my mate is everything I have ever desired for them to be. I thank you my mate is hungering and thirsting after righteousness." When they goof, you just tell God, "That's not like my mate."

DON'T ASSUME!! When you assume, you always assume the worst. Don't do it!! All it does is cause trouble. For example: If your husband has just given you a gift, and you happen to find receipts in his coat pocket for two identical gifts, don't assume one is for his ex-girlfriend.

I begged a lady in this situation, not to confront her husband with her evidence. She found out later he had gotten both her. and their married daughter the same gift. She was very thankful she hadn't accused him falsely. Their marriage had just been healed and it could have been disaster.

Remember, just because your mate has returned home, doesn't mean you quit praying, interceding, and reading the Word....You've Only Just Begun....

Chapter 11

~ ❧ ~

Some Questions You Have asked?

*W*hat are standers? Standers are simply believers who desire to honor their wedding vows. They believe God's Word that says death not divorce, dissolves a marriage. They believe marriage is a covenant with God, not a contract with a mate.

They are not standing for something, but because they are something...married until death. Ephesians 6:13 says, "Having done all to stand, stand!" So, that is what they are doing, standing.

What do you mean by a covenant? A covenant is a commitment or vow, dissolvable only by death, made to another party in the presence of God.

Your wedding vows were a covenant made to God. Keeping your vow is not dependent upon whether or not your mate keeps their vow. You both spoke your vows to God independently of each other. This covenant cannot be broken, just violated. In the same way, you cannot break the law, (it's still the law) you only violate it.

Malachi 2:14 is the verse that leaped off the page of a Gideon Bible the night Dana had decided to disappear. "The Lord has been witness between thee and the wife of thy youth, against whom thou hast dealt treacherously, yet is she thy companion and the wife of thy COVENANT." In Proverbs 2:17 it says,"The wayward wife has left the partner of her youth and ignored the COVENANT she made before God. These marriage covenants are non-cancelable.

The question that we are asked most frequently is, "But doesn't the Bible say that if your mate commits adultery you can divorce them?"

No, adultery is never ONCE given as a reason for divorce in the Bible. Fornication is, but not adultery. Back when Jesus said these words, He knew that if your mate committed adultery, divorce was unnecessary. You were soon to be a widow or widower by virtue of your mate being stoned to death, thus you were free to remarry.

The dictionary definition of adultery is voluntary sexual relations of a married person with any other than the lawful mate. Fornication is a sexual act between unmarried persons. Adultery and fornication appear in the same sentence six places in the Bible: Matthew 5:32, Matthew 15:19, Matthew 19:9, Mark 7:21, I Cor. 6:9, and Galations 5:19. They are definitely *not* the same word.

Jesus was telling those who were betrothed, that if they found out the person they were betrothed to had committed fornication with someone, they could divorce them. That is why Joseph said in Matthew 1:19 he did not want to expose Mary to public disgrace, (like stoning) he had in mind to divorce her quietly because she was with child before their marriage feast.

When you became betrothed, it was the same as being married, except the consummation came later (usually at least a year to make sure the bride was chaste).

After the wedding feast, the guests waited for the couple to consummate their marriage. The bridegroom would come out of the bridal room to show them the sheet with blood on it that proved she was a virgin.

The "Exception Clause" in Matthew, chapters five

and nineteen is not an "Exception Clause" that says you can remarry if your mate commits adultery. Jesus was saying a man could divorce his wife if there was no blood on the sheet, because that meant she had committed fornication.

So in the day of Jesus, you could get a divorce for fornication, not adultery. When we were in the Holy Land, a Jewish scholar from Hebrew University explained this in detail to us.

Jesus says in Luke 16:18, "Every man who divorces his wife and marries another woman is living with a woman who isn't his wife. And every man who marries a divorced woman is living with someone else's wife."

Jesus says in Mark 10:11, "Anyone who divorces his wife and marries another woman is sinning against his first wife by living with a woman who isn't his wife. And if a woman divorces her husband and marries another man, she is living with a man who isn't her husband" (Anderson Bible).

Why do you think John the Baptist lost his head? The answer is simple, it was because he told Herod, who had married his brother's wife, that he was committing adultery.

Is divorce an unforgivable sin that will keep me out of heaven? No! Nowhere in the Bible does the Word say divorce cannot be forgiven. It's like any other sin. You repent and forsake the sin. The problem is the conjunction, AND in the preceding sentence. You are to forsake the sin.

When you add AND marries to divorce, Jesus calls it adultery every time. When you take into account that the Word says several places in the Bible that no adulterer will enter the kingdom of God, it should make you count the cost.

What about Deut. 24:2-4 and remarrying your first wife? Deut. 24 says that if a man divorces a woman who then remarries, he is not to take her back again, for she has become corrupted. But Jeremiah 3:1 addresses the question of remarrying your mate. It says: "There is a law (referring to Deut. 24) that if a man divorces a woman who then remarries, he is not to take her back again, for she has become corrupted. But though YOU have left ME and married many lovers, yet I have invited you to come to me again, the Lord declares!!!"

God has made a clear statement here that even though we marry others, he wants us back as his bride. He is telling them that they didn't understand the meaning of Deut. 24, and He is clarifying it for them. And even though you might have divorced your first mate God said HE made you ONE and you will never again be two.

Hosea took Gomer back even though she was a harlot and had had many lovers. David reclaimed Michal, Saul's daughter after she married someone else II Samuel 3.

What can I do when my mate announces they are leaving and filing for divorce? What could you do if your husband or wife jumped out of an airplane without a parachute and they were floating through the air. NOT ONE THING!

You have to realize your mate is out of your control and only the divine intervention of God can save them. You surrender them to the Lord and quit trying to do what you think the Lord isn't getting done. You give them to the Lord the same way Abraham gave Isaac to the Lord when he took him up the mountain. It is not easy to do and requires much prayer and often times, fasting.

The day Dana told me he was getting a divorce and there was not a thing I could do about it, I paced the floor the entire day. I was agonizing in prayer, pleading with God to show me a way to stop him.

Finally, I realized the futility of this and I cried out

to the Lord in surrender, GOD, I GIVE UP!!! DO IT YOUR WAY. And HE did.

God says in Job 22:30 that though he is not innocent, he will be saved through the cleanness of your hands. I claimed this verse and had peace.

If God is all powerful, why doesn't He just snap his fingers and bring my mate home? Why do I have to go through this horrible experience? If God really loved me He would stop this divorce right now.

The answer is, WE ARE IN A WAR! In Ephesians 6:12 Paul states, "For we wrestle not against flesh and blood, but against principalities, against powers, against the rulers of darkness of this world, against spiritual wickedness in high places."

GOD KNOWS SOMETHING ABOUT YOUR SITUATION THAT YOU DON'T KNOW. He does love you, and His plans for you are for good not evil. He also knows that you cannot fight this battle of good against evil lying on beds of ease.

When soldiers prepare for battle, they don't stay in fancy hotels with room service, where their every want is instantly supplied. When soldiers prepare for battle, their training extends them beyond what they think they can endure. AND they don't tell the General how to run the army.

If you want to be a soldier in God's army, be prepared for boot camp. Paul's boot camp included receiving 39 lashes five times, being in prison; being beaten with rods three times, stoned, shipwrecked three times. He knew hunger and thirst and was in constant danger.

How do you survive? My daughter's advice to me was always the same no matter what I was going through. Mother, don't take anything personally Dad says or does. In everything give thanks for this is the will of God in Christ Jesus concerning you. And Mother, someday you will thank and praise God He allowed you to go through these trials. And she was right.

A good rule of thumb is, when you go through the valley of weeping, dig a well to the living water.

You mentioned fasting. What is that? Fasting is going without food for a certain length of time. You are telling the Lord, I would rather spend time with you, than to eat. Sometimes you hear Him tell you, I would like you to fast tomorrow, or I would like you to fast three days, or five days, or ten days. etc. It is not as difficult as it sounds. The benefits are worth the cost.

Why fast? Isaiah 58:6 tells us, also Joel 2:12. Ezra 8:21 says "Then I proclaimed a fast that we might afflict (humble) ourselves before our God, to seek of Him a right way for us...and He listened to our entreaty."

I have had many wonderful answers to my prayers when I fasted. I would recommend it as a way of life. Jesus fasted 40 days and HE did say, "WHEN YOU FAST."

What about that verse in I Corinthians 7 that says "But if the unbelieving depart, let him depart, a brother or a sister is not under bondage in such cases?" Doesn't that verse give me a right to remarry?

No, it doesn't. Paul is saying that if you have a mate who is an unbeliever and he doesn't want to live with you, you do not have to be under bondage to him. Let him go. But, in I Corinthians 7: 10 he says "and unto the married I command, yet not I, but the Lord. Let not the wife depart from her husband: But and if she depart, let her remain UNMARRIED OR BE RECONCILED TO HER HUSBAND.

In the same chapter, verse 39 Paul says the wife is bound by the law AS LONG AS HER HUSBAND LIVETH, but if her husband be dead, she is at liberty to be married to whom she will; only in the Lord. Paul is saying, just in case you misunderstood about the bondage, let me say it this way, you are married until one of you dies. It is *not* divorce, but death that ends a marriage.

How was my born-again, spirit-filled mate able to "Cross the line" and commit adultery? I just can't understand how that could happen.

They had to open the door to Satan. Satan sets a snare, or trap, but in order for Satan's trap to snap shut, it has to be stepped on Amos 3:5.

Sometimes it happens because they entertain a lustful thought instead of rejecting it. They are saying if the right opportunity came along, I just might go for it. Soon, the devil makes sure the right opportunity comes along.

One of Satan's favorite methods to get a believer into deception and finally into delusion, is to tell them, "Everybody (including Christians) is doing it, so it has to be okay."

How can I go on living? Realize that nothing will destroy you, but your own attitude. Peace of mind is independent from what is happening to us. You can choose your own emotions. It isn't what happens to you, it's how you react to what happens to you. You are the person you are 10% because of what has happened to you, and 90% because of the way you have reacted to what has happened to you. You can choose victory or defeat. You can choose to be a victim or a victor. You can choose hope or hopelessness. Troubles are not an option in our life, but misery is. Problems are not an option in our life, but bitterness is.

Our despair comes out of the fact we overrule what God's Word say. I Thess. 5:18 says, **"In everything give thanks: for this is the will of God in Christ Jesus concerning you."**

Our circumstances are the only method Satan has ever used to destroy us. We know that God shapes every circumstance for our good, and what Satan means for our harm God turns for our good so, "Let gratitude be your attitude." You can't be destroyed with a thankful heart.

How will I ever make it financially? We struggled with finances most of our life until one day Dana said, "You know I believe God loves a grateful people, I am going to praise Him that whatever He sends us, *it is enough* from now on." He started doing that several years ago and God has never disappointed us.

But sometimes there is a need to reevaluate the choices you make financially. Don't blame God when your wants have replaced your needs. With wisdom, little can be much, without wisdom much can be little. Financial discipline is a must. God is not obligated to subsidize bad management.

You can make a choice where you shop for clothes, what brand of food you buy, whether you cook at home or eat out, between cable TV or not. You can choose what time of day you make phone calls. Never tell your children, "We can't afford this", tell them we choose to spend our money differently.

Are you giving 10 % of your income to the Lord as He tells you to do? You cannot rob God and then ask Him to bless your finances. That would be like stealing your neighbor's car and then asking him if he would please wax it for you. Avoid easy-outs, quick riches, hasty decisions. Turn no corner quickly, but in prayer and supplication let your requests be made known to God. AND, thank God that whatever He sends you is enough.

We owed our creditors $80,000 when our marriage turned around. One day I was lamenting to a friend that I had no money to pay all the creditors who would call and demand their money.

My friend asked me the question, How do you eat an elephant?" I replied, "I don't have any idea." Their answer to me was, "One bite at a time"! What a revelation! So, we paid the debt one bite at a time.

How many people should I talk to about my situation? The less people you talk to about it the better. It really helps to have a prayer partner who listens, but doesn't sympathize. We have a saying, "Sympathy kills, compassion gives life".

When you repeat over and over what has happened to you to a lot of people, you feed your injuries. And what you feed grows. Soon you are into "Poor me" and "It's all THEIR fault." When you love someone, you do not want them to look bad in other people's eyes, especially your children's eyes.

Why am I made out to be the villain? They are the ones who have deserted their family, committed adultery, lied, and are not providing for their family. According to John 3: 20, it is because "Everyone who does evil hates the light, and will not come into the light for fear that his deeds will be exposed."

Proverbs 26:28 says that they hate you in direct proportion to how much they have hurt you. They are acting perfectly normal for someone controlled by Satan. You can't talk to them, so **pray** it, don't say it.

A stander called crying, "I can't believe what just happened". Her husband's live-in girlfriend had just called. She demanded that the stander quit dragging her feet and allow this divorce to go through. The girlfriend had already divorced her pastor-husband and wanted to marry this man.

She gave as her reason, "Your husband and I have a ministry together and it doesn't look good for us not to be married." When confronted by the wife that this was adultery and was sin, the answer came back, but God's Grace covers our sin.

You cannot reason with a person who is in deception. You pray the Word. This type of situation is what Jude is talking about in verse four, when he says, "Men use Grace as a license for immorality." or in more modern day terms, "People are using Grace as their license to sin." But God is not buying this deception.

People call in and say, but, "They" seem to have

everything going for them. It isn't fair. I can barely put food on the table for myself and kids, and he takes off for Europe with his "Friend."

One lady whose husband divorced her after 35 years put it this way: "She" has stolen my husband, my children, my father and mother in-law, my sister and brother in-law and their children, my standard of living, my trips, our friends, my security, my holidays.

But the thing that makes me absolutely furious is, "She" gets the nice presents my in-laws used to give to me at Christmas." A lot of you can relate to that statement.

The Bible says in Job 27:18, "Every house built by the wicked is as fragile as a spider's web." Psalm 73 is a good psalm to read if you are feeling envious that the wicked seem to prosper. Obadiah 1:15 says, "Your acts will boomerang upon your heads." In other words, "What goes around comes around."

Do I fight for my rights? The question is who is your provider? Count the cost. If you struggle for finances, how much of it goes to attorneys, etc.? More can be done through prayer and praise than through lawyers. "I trust you Father to take care of me, I thank you, Father, that YOU are my lawyer, etc." Sometimes you can win the battle and lose the war. We do tell people to get a lawyer **after** they receive their divorce papers, so they can slow the process down.

What happens if you have been waiting a long time for your mate to come home and you feel like you have been put on "Hold"? You believe you have done everything God has told you to do and still, no results?

Would you quit waiting for a child to come home if he had been kidnapped? Well, your mate has been kidnapped by Satan. Intercessory prayer is the key that unlocks the door. You NEVER, NEVER, NEVER, give up. Just keep on keeping on.

Remember and never forget, the sin that kept Israel

out of the promised land for forty years was murmuring. Sometimes we need to search our hearts and make sure we are not murmuring against God. Everything you say and do should bring glory to the Father.

But shouldn't I deliver an ultimatum to my husband or wife if they are living at home but spending several nights a week in adultery at their friend's home?

We have not talked to one person who delivered an ultimatum and the mate chose to stay at home. When a person is in deception, there is no point of reference with which to connect.

Let me tell you the story of Rhonda. Her husband had gone back and forth between her and his girlfriend, Helen for nearly three years. He would tell Rhonda, "I love you, but I just can't break-off this affair."

One evening Rhonda called, sobbing uncontrollably. I could barely understand her words. "Next month is Don's and my twenty-fifth wedding anniversary. He just called to tell me he was going to be gone over our anniversary. He and Helen have planned a trip abroad and he said there was no way the date could be changed so he could be home. He said he was terribly sorry to hurt me, but he just had to go."

Rhonda sent him off with, "Have a good time." Inwardly she was hoping he would be miserable. She knew nothing she could say to him would make him change his mind, so why say anything. She just prayed, Father I thank you my husband loves me so much.

Her friends and family would ask her, "Why don't you ever say anything bad about Don?" Her answer was always the same, "Why should I? I love him for who he is, not for what he does."

Don and his "Friend" got into a big fight on their trip when Don spent a lot of money on presents for his wife, children and grandchildren. (As I'm writing this, I'm saying to myself, "This is unbelievable.)"

Helen delivered an ultimatum and Don went home

to his wife. Rhonda explained that God had answered her prayers when Don wept and wept and became a broken man. Like the Prodigal Son he asked himself, "What am I doing with this woman, when I have a wife at home who loves me the way Rhonda loves me."

He has been home nearly a year now and Rhonda's voice was exuberant on the phone as she exclaimed, "If I was any happier, I couldn't stand it."

What do people mean when they tell me to, "Get on with your Life"? The answer to that question is, "Go find somebody else. Forget all your memories of the good times, and bad. Forget your past relationship as though the commitment you made in your wedding vows was meaningless. Go for it. You deserve to be happy. Forget that some people say marriage is for life, they don't know what they are talking about. There are so many wonderful pastors and elders, and musicians in second marriages and God is blessing them, so it has to be okay with God".

No, it isn't!!! God says he hates divorce. Jesus says in Matthew 19:5,6 that a man should leave his father and mother, and be FOREVER united to his wife. The two shall become one—NO LONGER two, but one. And no man may divorce what God has joined together.

People say, "But, I'm a new person in Christ, he will not hold me accountable for what I did before I knew him." Try telling that to a banker who holds your mortgage on your home. Tell him, "I'm a new person, and you can't hold me accountable for anything I signed, said or agreed to do before I accepted Christ."

He will inform you, "I'm sorry, but you are accountable for what you agreed to do and you will pay what you owe." The Lord shows us in His Word, men are not to set aside their vows.

What are my options after my mate divorces me? The word say in I Corinthians 7:11 your options are to either remain unmarried, or else be reconciled.

Several things will determine how you wait for your mate's return. You can turn to bitterness, anger, and all the other destructive self-defending thought patterns, or you can walk in forgiveness and be liberated by trusting the Lord. You then are free to love your mate, expecting nothing in return. You are free to walk in peace when Jesus becomes your confidant, your comforter, your friend, your Saviour, and your "All in All." You can enjoy all the good things of life that God has made available to you without comparing your circumstances with your mates.

I cried every day for almost a year, and I asked the Lord, "Will, I ever have a day I don't cry?" Psalm 84:5- 6 talks about Baca, the Valley of Weeping. "Blessed (are those) whose strength is in thee;...Who passing through the valley of Baca make it a well." So, we dig a well when we go through the valley of weeping and drink God's Living Water. We find God is sufficient to take us through our pain. And yes, you will laugh again. I did.

I laugh a lot now, but I remember how it felt to hear somebody laugh when I was hurting so badly the laughter seemed almost more than I could bear.

One lady called us the other day, and said, "I finally understand what you are talking about when you say you can get on with your life. I am still waiting for my husband to come home, but I am enjoying life. I have so much to be thankful for." We had been telling her over and over again, "You don't have to put your life on hold. You are free to live a fulfilled life."

What she did was to think about the positive instead of entertaining the negative. You don't forget the pain, you just don't let the pain control you. Settle Psalm 112:7 in your mind. "He, (God's child) does not fear bad news, nor live in dread of what may happen", because we know God shapes every circumstance for our good.

We believe the prophecy to be true that was placed on our list of marriages, "Where there is faith, God WILL perform." So, it is up to HIM to perform, and up to us to have faith. Jesus touched them, and they were healed. Will HE do any less for you?

**GOD STILL SHAPES EVERY
CIRCUMSTANCE FOR MY GOOD!**

Chapter 12

―❧❦❧―

Val's Prayers

I Praise and Thank You Father

That: **My husband loves me so much.**

That: **My marriage is healed.**

That: **You are not in the marriage-breaking-up-business.**

That: **You have given me a supernatural love for my mate.**

That: **You are perfecting that which concerns me.**

That: **You do not owe me an explanation for what happens in my life.**

That: **I desire to desire your desires in my life.**

That: **All true joy is born of sorrow.**

That: **You'll never make a mistake in my life.**

That: **It is your will to heal my marriage, because according to Malachi 2:16 you hate divorce.**

That: **Those who have faith you will perform. (Prophecy on our list of marriages)**

That: **Divorce is no option for me as a believer, because divorce is a form of unforgiveness.**

That: **I don't have to be right. I can't afford the luxury of strife and self-pity.**

That: **I am not to be my own tormentor.**

That: **Your promise given is kept.**

That: According to Ephesians 5:33 amplified, I will respect and reverence my husband. I will notice him, honor him, prefer him, venerate and esteem him, defer to him, praise him, and love and admire him exceedingly.

That: Since I KNOW my marriage is healed, I will disregard the symptoms and walk beyond my sight.

That: From glory to glory You're changing me. II Cor. 3:18

That: Your Word says I can ask you to place a wall of fire around my mate and the Glory within. Zech. 2:5

That: All ungodly ties and counsel have been broken.

That: YOU have given us the Word in Jeremiah 31:16 "Refrain your voice from weeping and your eyes from tears, for I shall reward your works and he shall return back from the land of the enemy and there is hope for you."

That: I know that someday I will praise Your Name that You allowed me to go through this.

That: According to II Chronicles 20:15, this battle is not mine, but YOURS.

That: You are perfecting that which concerns me. Psalm 138:8. Forgive me Father, when I, me, my, mine, is more important to me than preferring my mate.

That: I can praise you that this season of sin my mate is in, is no longer pleasurable to them. Thank you that I really have no other option than to stand for my marriage, Father.

That: There is no marriage too hard for you to heal when I stand on God's Word.

That: You are making me into the woman or man God planned for me to be and into the husband or wife my mate has always prayed I would be.

That: I don't need to see to believe my marriage is healed. I need to believe to see.

That: I can trust you. Nothing happens to me that doesn't come through Your hands first.

That: Divorce is never final. Man cannot separate what God has joined together.

That: Sorrows are too precious to be wasted. (Mrs. Charles Cowman) Praise you that sorrows lift us to higher ground.

That: I don't need to worry about finances. Praise you whatever you send is enough and some left over.

That: God shapes every circumstance for my good.

That: You are always available. When we call upon your name, you NEVER put us on hold.

That: You always bring beauty from ashes.

That: According to Obadiah 1:15 "What goes around comes around. I don't need to seek revenge because Colossians 3:25 tells me, "He who does wrong will receive the consequences of the wrong which he has done."

That: You know something about my situation I don't know. You have the total picture, I don't.

That: The veil is being torn from my mates eyes. The deception is being exposed and he (she) now sees TRUTH.

That: You turn people around in the middle of the night while they sleep, keeping them from the pit. Job 33:24

That: My mate has been set free from the snare of the fowler.

That: Satan is defeated by the blood of Jesus and the Word of my testimony. I plead the blood of Jesus over my mate, and do now testify that he (she) has been set free from Satan's control.

That: My husband (wife) has a broken, contrite, and penitent spirit.

That: According to Hosea 2:15, God says He will transform our Valley of Troubles into a door of Hope.

That: When I cried out, "I give up, God. Do it your way," HE DID.

That: "Blessed is the man (woman) who trusts in the Lord, whose HOPE the Lord is." Jeremiah 17:7

That: Hope does not disappoint us. Romans 5:5

FOR I KNOW THE PLANS I HAVE FOR YOU, SAYS THE LORD. THEY ARE PLANS FOR GOOD AND NOT FOR EVIL, TO GIVE YOU A FUTURE AND A HOPE Jeremiah 29:11 Living Bible.

Don't Forget

*D*on't forget to release your mate from the demand that they are responsible for your happiness and fulfillment. The joy of the Lord is your strength. It's not what happens to you, it's how you react to what happens to you.

Don't forget that the obvious is not the problem. We are not fighting flesh and blood, but we are fighting against principalities, against powers, against the rulers of the darkness of this world. Your mate is not your enemy. Satan is your enemy.

Don't forget that when you contact your mate, you don't demand a response. It threatens them and pushes them away. Your PRIMARY prayer is for their salvation. Let the Holy Spirit convict them. When God's Holy Spirit convicts, HE brings repentance. When we convict, WE bring rebellion.

Don't forget to read God's Word every day. He tells us in Isaiah 26:3, "God will keep you in perfect peace if you stay your mind on HIM."

DON'T FORGET — GOD'S WORD GIVEN IS KEPT!